las
tha

$\sqrt{}$

$-1.$

THREE BODLEY HEAD MONOGRAPHS

GENERAL EDITOR: KATHLEEN LINES

THREE BODLEY HEAD MONOGRAPHS

Hugh Lofting
EDWARD BLISHEN

Geoffrey Trease
MARGARET MEEK

J. M. Barrie
ROGER LANCELYN GREEN

THE BODLEY HEAD
LONDON SYDNEY
TORONTO

SBN 370 00882 0

Hugh Lofting © Edward Blishen 1968
Geoffrey Trease © Margaret Meek 1960
J. M. Barrie © Roger Lancelyn Green 1960
Printed and bound in Great Britain for

The Bodley Head Ltd

9 Bow Street, London WC2
by C. Tinling & Co. Ltd, Prescot
Set in Monotype Ehrhardt
'Hugh Lofting' first published 1968
*'Geoffrey Trease' and 'J. M. Barrie' first published, in
two individual volumes, 1960*
This edition, revised and re-set, 1968

Hugh Lofting

EDWARD BLISHEN

CONTENTS

i Hugh Lofting: His Life, 9

ii The World of Doctor Dolittle, 19

iii Other Works, 42

iv The Illustrator, 50

v A Summing Up, 54

Bibliography, 61

1. Hugh Lofting: His Life

Hugh Lofting was an original, whose life nevertheless falls into no exceptional pattern of literary biography. Like his own creation, John Dolittle MD, he appears to have been a largely self-effacing man: or, to put it another way, one content to express himself mainly through his work. On the occasions when he burst into print (and the phrase is justified) in his own person, rather than through fiction, it was to express large radical ideas, a passionate longing for international sanity, that dominated his life after his experiences in the trenches of France and Flanders in the First World War. There is an actual sense in which one learns more about Lofting from the books he wrote about the adventures of Doctor Dolittle than from such biographical facts as emerge. And as with so many outstanding writers for children—that is, those who saw in children their true and principal audience—the essence of much of his life work was contained, one guesses, in the nature of his own childhood.

He was born on January 14, 1886, at Maidenhead, in Berkshire, of an Irish father, John Brien Lofting, and an English mother, Elizabeth Agnes: both were Roman Catholics. There were six in the family: five boys and a girl. He had a 'strange affinity for animals', his younger son has said of him, and this appeared very early. Indeed, in an anecdote from his childhood we can perhaps detect the source of Doctor Dolittle himself. One of the Doctor's qualities was that he cared for animals at the cost of all domestic convenience—and so, it seems, did the young

Lofting; for, until it was discovered, he kept in his mother's linen closet what has been described as 'a combination zoo and natural history museum'. He adored dogs (when he was an adult there were usually three or four in the house), but had no great liking for cats. Already—with his family as audience—he was given to story-telling: and already his heart was set on being a writer.

Doctor Dolittle's indifference to domestic life (except in so far as it ought to provide a 'marvellous kitchen' in which you could stretch and talk without having to care too much about the furniture) may reflect Lofting's own very small experience of home life as a child. For at the age of eight he was sent to a boarding school—a Jesuit college, Mount St Mary, in Chesterfield, Derbyshire—and thereafter he is said to have seen his family only occasionally. Father James Scholes, a school fellow, remembers Lofting as a slightly-built boy, not good at games. The records of Lofting's school career are thin, but searching among them made the present Rector, Philip A. Wetz SJ, reflect on 'the unique place the school was in those days'.

'It was rather like a very large family (120 boys), strict in religious observance, not very interested in the world outside but absorbed with its own activities, joys and sorrows. The School was almost the entire boy's life, and the staff had very little interest beside the good of the boys spiritually, morally and educationally; they devoted their time not merely to the betterment of the boys but also to seeing that their lives were punctuated by outings, special days, and especially plays and concerts. A boy was in fact brought up in an atmosphere almost impossible to communicate to others, and which I can glimpse only by constant contact with one or two who were brought up under this paternalistic and devoted treatment.'

This was the enclosed and protected world in which Lofting spent ten years of his life. Only two precise details about that period are discoverable at this distance of time: one trivial—that he passed his Oxford Junior Locals examination in 1901: the other a little startling—that in the same year, at the age of fifteen, he played the leading role of the Burgomaster, Mathias, in that arch-melodrama, *The Bells*, in which Sir Henry Irving had scored one of his greatest successes a few years before.

Despite his lack of flair at games, he is remembered as an active boy, with a love of mountain climbing and fishing. (To these pastimes in later life he added ski-ing and golf.)

It is not clear whether he had yet expressed a desire to try to earn his living as a writer. However that may be, it was his father's ruling for all the Lofting boys that each should train for some profession on which he could fall back if other choices of a career came to nothing. A longing to wander the world seems to have chimed in here with a family tradition and to have determined Lofting to become a civil engineer, with an architectural bias. In 1904 he took the first step, going to America to begin his studies at the Massachusetts Institute of Technology. He returned to England a year later and completed the course at the London Polytechnic.

Already, embryonically, the pattern of his life was set. America was for a large part of that life to be his physical home, although the scene of his writing was, curiously, always to remain English. He was already, as a student, turning out short stories and plays. At the age of twenty-two, now qualified, and after a very brief period devoted to architecture, he went to Canada, prospecting (the experience is reflected in *The Puddleby Gold Rush*) and surveying. Between 1910 and 1912 he worked as an engineer for the

Lagos Railway in West Africa and the United Railways of Havana. He hated every moment of it, his son Christopher has said, and considered himself a very bad engineer.

His wanderlust now seemed to be satisfied, and the urge to write took its place. In 1912 he returned to the United States, married Flora Small, of New York, gave up engineering and began contributing articles and short stories to magazines. Much of this early work was broad burlesque—pun-ridden comedy of a kind that remained a permanent thread in his writing. But for the First World War it seems possible that he would have settled to the life of a humorous journalist. For a while, after the outbreak of war, he worked for the British Ministry of Information in New York, but in 1916 he joined the Irish Guards. He saw service in France and Flanders, and in 1917 was wounded and invalided out of the Army.

It was in the trenches that the vital event of his life had occurred. He had to write home; but what, from that infernal scene, could he say to his children, Elizabeth and Colin?

'My children at home wanted letters from me—and they wanted them with illustration rather than without. There seemed very little of interest to write to youngsters from the front; the news was either too horrible or dull. And it was all censored. One thing, however, that kept forcing itself more and more on my attention was the very considerable part the animals were playing in the world war and that as time went on they, too, seemed to become Fatalists . . .

'If we made the animals take the same chances we did ourselves, why did we not give them similar attention when wounded? But obviously to develop a horse-surgery as good as that of our Casualty Clearing Station would necessitate a knowledge of horse language . . .'

And that, Lofting said, was the beginning of the idea of

Doctor Dolittle. He was to be 'an eccentric country physician with a bent for natural history and a great love of pets, who finally decides to give up his human practice for the more difficult, more sincere and, for him, more attractive therapy of the animal kingdom. He is challenged by the difficulty of the work—for obviously it requires a much cleverer brain to become a good animal doctor (who must first acquire all animal languages and physiologies) than it does to take care of the mere human hypochondriac.'

His narrative letters delighted his children, and Colin (snub-nosed like the Doctor, and indeed like all Lofting's heroes) insisted on being known as John Dolittle. In 1919, when the family returned to America, Lofting had already decided, at his wife's prompting, to turn the letters into a book. But an encounter with an established writer on the boat going home may have been decisive. Cecil Roberts, the novelist, recalled that on that Atlantic crossing he made the acquaintance of a man who invariably sat in the deck chair next to his own.

'Every evening about six he said he had to disappear to read a bedtime story to Dr Dolittle. I inquired who Dr Dolittle was and he said it was his little son. The next day a snub-nosed boy appeared on deck with his mother and thus I made the acquaintance of the original Dr Dolittle. Later Hugh Lofting at my request showed me some of his manuscript and he wondered if it would make a book. I was at once struck by the quality of the stories and, enthusiastic about their publication, recommended him to my publisher, Mr Stokes . . .'

The family settled in Madison, Connecticut, and in 1920 *The Story of Doctor Dolittle* appeared. It was an instant success, and was followed by *The Voyages of Doctor Dolittle* in 1922. Hugh Walpole, whose critical approval at the time was worth much, picked up a copy of *The Story* when on a visit to America, fell under its spell, and contributed a foreword to later editions in which he acclaimed the book as a classic of the quality of *Alice in Wonderland*. This judgement was echoed by the Newbery Medal Awards Committee in April, 1923, when they selected *The Voyages* as the medal-winner for that year. Reflecting on this award, Bertha Miller has said that the committee 'wished to recognise the originality and skill which has gone into the making of *The Story of Doctor Dolittle*, which even at that date they believed to be a classic'.* Altogether, Hugh Lofting had arrived, and he settled down to mine this copious vein of fantasy that he had opened up. Thereafter, his life was very much that of the professional writer with an assured audience, intermitted with visits to schools, libraries and clubs.

He had by now a firm grasp on two principles that remained of the very first importance to him for the rest of his life, and that determined the quality of all his work. They followed one from the other. The first was that he must never write down to children. 'What the intelligent child likes,' he once said, 'is being "written up" to. He wants promotion, he wants to get on in the adult world.' This was not a common perception among writers for children in the 1920s; perhaps it has never become very common. A story, he believed, should be good for any reader, whatever his age. He must write so straightforwardly and entertainingly that a child would immediately understand him; unfamiliar or difficult expressions children would take in their stride, if the context were sufficiently clear and simple. He detested the phrase 'a book for juveniles'. It was as absurd, he said (in a typical turn of wit), as to describe a book as being for

* Bertha Miller, *Newbery Medal Books 1922–1955*, p. 17.

'seniles'. He always took with enormous seriousness the letters he received from children, and was delighted when they contained queries about the Doctor's biography that made it clear that children thought of Dolittle as an actual person.

The second principle he established for himself was more remarkable. He believed with passion that story books for the young could either inflame race hatreds or 'educate them out' of children. This idea he expressed with great vehemence in articles that appeared in the *Nation* in 1923 and 1924.

'An ingrained admiration for tin-soldierdom,' he wrote, 'seems as yet to be part of every child's metamorphosis . . . Many zealous advocates of internationalism complain that their small boys, who have heard nothing in the home in praise of war since they were born, insist when they reach a certain age on making wooden swords, marching up and down the garden, and smiting off the heads of dandelion enemies.

'The reason for this is not very far to seek. The boy may not have heard his father boasting of the genius of a crack regiment, but he has read a whole heap of so-called children's classics in which highly painted heroes galloped, glorious and victorious, across bloody battlefields. That kind of battlefield has gone for good—it is still bloody, but you don't gallop. And since that kind of battlefield has gone, that kind of book—for children—should go too . . .

'The trouble with all heroes and all heroic games has been that they were always selectively reported. Both sides were very seldom fairly given of either the man or the games. Yet truthfulness, realism, is a prominent characteristic of modern writing, and you can make a hero out of anyone, e.g. Potash and Perlmutter. There's no misrepresentation there. Yet people love them . . .

'In the determination of his aesthetic leanings and sociological opinions the force of emulation from a boy's books is almost as potent as that from his living heroes and companions . . .'

In his stubborn mufti, rejecting honours, at war with fox-hunting and with war itself, John Dolittle is plainly an attempt to create, for children, a new, more rational and gentle hero for them to emulate. But in his attack on literature for children that glorifies war or glamorises violence, Lofting goes further, and incidentally makes it clear why, though he had a gift for romantic writing, he rarely gave it its head.

'If one were to suggest that all the war-hero books that are outdated be closed to ages under twenty, one would probably be met with opposition from still another quarter. This, the romantic curator of the folk-tale. Those dear people who, blinded by the need of antique glamour in an ugly utilitarian world, would raise the child upon the sagas.

'The beauty of the sagas is something none of us would like to see disappear. Yet their aesthetic burden includes many things beside beauty. Bloodthirstiness, superstition, bigotry, and primitive ignorance are among these. Of a great deal of this lore of old stories and rhymes which we hand down to our children the only virtue allowable is that it is old—that it was handed down to us . . .'

And Lofting defines what was, in fact, his own increasingly desperate aim in his writing for children:

'If we make children see that all races, given equal physical and mental chances for development, have about the same batting averages* of good and bad, we shall have laid another very substantial foundation stone in the edifice of peace and internationalism.'

* It is curiously touching to note this very English phrase. Americans will forgive me for saying that Hugh Lofting, for all his years of residence, never really became an American. (He kept, all his life, his British citizenship.)

Lofting's polemical journalese may come as a surprise to those who know only his style as a children's storyteller; but that it might do so is perhaps a tribute to the exuberant inventiveness, humour and ingenuity with which, in his stories, he clothed his own endeavour to achieve these aims. Here, in his own voice, is the angry, fervent man who raised on the foundations of his idealistic ardour such an edifice of gentle, comic fiction.

His happiest work, as we shall see later in this study, was produced between 1920 and 1927. In the latter year a dramatisation by Harcourt Williams of episodes from the Dolittle stories, under the title *Doctor Dolittle's Play*, was presented in Miss Jean Sterling Mackinlay's season in London, and drew full audiences of children to whom John Dolittle was no mere fiction. But also in that year his first wife died. He married again in 1928, his bride being Katherine Harrower-Peters; but she too died very shortly after their marriage in the influenza epidemic of that year. His health had begun to fail, and he was tiring of Doctor Dolittle. 'He tried to get rid of him,' his son Christopher has said, 'by sending him to the Moon. (But like Conan Doyle with Sherlock Holmes, he had to bring him back.)' The enormous energies that had produced seven of the Dolittle books in as many years began to weaken. The Doctor was restored to life with *Doctor Dolittle's Return*, which appeared in 1933; but the last Dolittle, *Doctor Dolittle and the Secret Lake*, took thirteen years to complete, though part of the text and some of the drawings were printed in a syndicated feature in the *New York Herald-Tribune*.

In 1935 Lofting married again, his third wife being Josephine Fricker, of Toronto, whom he met while on a lecture tour. A son, Christopher, was born the following year in Topanga, California, where Lofting was then living.

It seems certain that poor health was not the sole reason for Lofting's failing energy as a writer. He was certainly never entirely well; his old war wound gave him trouble from time to time, and in his early forties he suffered from severe ulcers that slowly destroyed his remaining health. It may be because he was struggling with physical pain and exhaustion, as much as because of his essentially reserved nature, that people remember him (in the words of his English publisher, Mr G. Wren Howard of Jonathan Cape) as 'rather quiet and shy, shut up inside himself'. (Though it is perhaps important to place alongside those words others used by someone who knew him more closely: his sister-in-law, Miss Olga Fricker, who speaks of the pleasure he gave to his friends by his 'charm and whimsy'.) But to the effects of ill-health one must add the effects of the gradual worsening of world affairs. Having that passionate longing for international sanity that he expressed so strongly in his *Nation* articles, and that haunts especially the later Dolittle books, he cannot have found the 1930s anything but a mounting torture; and the horror and despair caused him by the outbreak of the Second World War are reflected in *Victory for the Slain*, his only serious published poem, which appeared in 1942. He saw the war out, writing little more; and died at Santa Monica, California, on September 27, 1947, at the age of 61.

11. The World of Doctor Dolittle

Lofting was, in a literary sense, a fortunate man. His first book was founded on an invention that is not merely ingenious (and one he had the gift to build on, for much of a writing lifetime) but that also enabled him to express what he wished to say about the world, without stint or dilution or camouflage, to the very audience to whom he thought it most worth saying.

The Dolittle books are a growth rather than a coolly planned series. They change in character and deepen as the author increases his grip on his original invention and ploughs into the books more and more of himself. When *The Story of Doctor Dolittle* appeared in 1920, as we have seen, it was welcomed by Hugh Walpole as the first children's classic since *Alice in Wonderland*; and the American committee that three years later awarded Lofting the Newbery Medal for his second book echoed this comparison. But, as we can now judge who possess the sequence whole, the comparison was misleading. *Alice* (and *The Wind in the Willows*, which the Newbery judges also mentioned) are classics of, as it were, perfection and completeness: we know where they begin and end. The Dolittle stories form a classic of another kind: in their rambling amplitude, their very unevenness, they are like life itself, and children can live in them, in a most generous sense. Indeed, as anyone knows who has read them through, and especially in the company of children, they merge into one another, confusingly. As with life, their interest is of a kind difficult to exhaust; but it can also be exhausting. The books lean on one another, contain contradictions, and abound in miscellaneous material. The very period which they cover is in doubt. There is no possibility of making a rational pattern out of such dates as swim to the surface; they dart about from somewhere round the opening of the nineteenth century, when Jip, the dog, knew George Morland, the portrait painter (1763–1804), to a date vaguely indicated by the sparrow Cheapside's reference to 'them old Crimea War veterans'. (At that period, Jip was still alive, the oldest of dogs; but by then, by similar internal evidence, John Dolittle must have been well over a hundred.) This vagueness of time is part of the magic of the Dolittle world, and seems unlikely to have been due to carelessness. The sense of the Doctor as an immortal is established by the typical device of being at once precise and improbable in this matter of dates.

One sees what drew Hugh Walpole to *The Story*; that book launched the *idea* of Doctor Dolittle—of the eccentric small-town doctor who turned from human medicine to the welfare of animals and, on the grounds of the enchanting argument that no patient can be well-served by a doctor to whom he cannot speak, set to and learned the languages of animals. And this idea, as Marcus Crouch has observed,* is one of the few really original ideas in children's fiction. In *The Story* there is already much of Lofting's quality. Here is his gift for curious invention that is always on the brink of whimsicality, but rarely drops into it. His imagination is at once extravagant and practical; and the practical quality in it turns the pushmi-pullyu, for example (the creature presented to the Doctor by the monkeys in gratitude for his treatment of their sickness), which might have been only a mildly funny fantasy animal, into something more. The pushmi-pullyu could have used both his heads

---

* *Treasure Seekers and Borrowers* (The Library Association, 1962).

for talking, but did not do so since that would have squandered his special advantage of eating and talking at one and the same time without impoliteness. At that single and typical stroke, the pushmi-pullyu is raised above whimsy and becomes a permanent delight in the memory, preserved by Lofting's very special practical wit. This was to be the character of so many of his inventions; they are preposterous, and yet Lofting presents them with such a reasonable air that fantasy seems as well-founded as any ordinary fact of the everyday world. Part of his special appeal to children is due to this element, indeed child-like, of the ridiculous notion soberly justified.

Yet *The Story* was, if not a false start, then one that set the tone for the series simply by showing Lofting what it should not be. In it, he is writing down for children, as he never did again: the turns of language have a cosy, simple quality that makes a reader constantly aware that he is not to take the story seriously. It is the language of the conscious tall story for children: carrying still, perhaps, the tone of the original oral tales told by Lofting to his son Colin. There is other evidence that Lofting has not yet established his grip on the opportunity offered to him by his invention of Doctor Dolittle. Flaws are found of an odd kind for a man whose lifelong obsession was the need for tolerance between living things. It may be that in the 1960s we are more sensitive to the colour question than even radicals of Lofting's order were in the 1920s, simply because its consequences are now on all our doorsteps; but such an explanation hardly covers his treatment of the episode in which the African Prince Bumpo pleads to have the hue of his face changed from black to white. This is so much at odds with the philosophy Lofting spent his life expressing that one suspects that the facetious elements in this first book, and in the tradition of story-telling that it subscribes to, led him astray. He had invented a set of sketchily comic Africans belonging to an order of comedy that rather easily leads to insensitive joking. Call a Prince, Bumpo; call his tribe the Jollijinki; and a writer is on his way to a perilously indiscriminate and patronising broadness of humour.

Interestingly, when Lofting changed course in the second book, and thereafter, he retained many of the elements of this facetious tradition of writing, but rarely let them lead him again so far from his fundamental purpose of promoting the idea of respect and tolerance between living things. He grasped, one suspects, the significance and use, for him, of those elements: which lay, as I shall argue in a moment, in their anti-romantic quality.

If he started off on several wrong feet in *The Story*, he also started off on several marvellously right ones. The Doctor himself was already keenly focused, though he, who was to be so richly and circumstantially documented, was there only in relatively thin outline, and certainly lacked many of the subtler qualities he was later to be given. (The Doctor ends the story in what, looking back, one sees to be a quite uncharacteristic posture, satisfied with riches; although already his scorn for money is established, and the fortune that he acquires at the end of *The Story* falls into his lap and is not sought. In all the later books, splendidly, money slips off his lap as fast as it lands there.) There is already the exhilarating sense, present in so many of the books, of a world in which long daring voyages are undertaken at the drop of a hat—each in spirit a fantastic magnification of any child's day of adventure and makebelieve in field or street, or by pond or stream, to be ended with tea back at home, as all the Dolittle stories were ended. The Doctor's animal household is almost complete, and Sarah

Dolittle, his sister, so brusquely driven from it when she complains about having a crocodile in the bath, has already made that brief appearance that is to be alluded to so often throughout the series, in a manner that makes Sarah a kind of touchstone of stuffy respectability: on the few occasions when, later, the Doctor actually blunders into her and her parsonical husband, it is always when John Dolittle is behaving in a more than usually unconventional fashion.

But the books that followed *The Story* immediately and enormously extended the range of the Dolittle world. The change is, first, one of tone. This is not merely a matter of Tommy Stubbins taking over as narrator; there is also a total change of manner. The accent, as it were, of the jolly and amusing uncle talking down to an audience of children is replaced by one that, fundamentally, is that of the serious memoir. The sentences grow longer; the restricted vocabulary of the first book is forgotten. The whole intent now is to suggest the reality of this world, to have it taken seriously by taking it seriously. This means, paradoxically, no loss of gaiety, but an increase in it. The fun of *The Story* was the fun of a confessed joke; all the fun of the following books derives its special rich quality from the suggestion, to which young readers readily submit, that we are not really joking at all.

To my mind the biggest change, to which I have already alluded, lies in his sudden confident handling of the facetious elements in his writing. These are found, from the very beginning, in the conception of the Doctor himself. Clumsy, 'round as a bee', enormous-booted, he is an overgrown boy in the dress of a Victorian general practitioner. The idea of marriage fills him with horror, he giggles when he is kissed. All this is, in origin, a projection of a boy's taste, and a facetious one. So, too, are the names: Bumpo, Matthew

Mugg, Tripsitinka, the Jollijinki. In *The Story*, such names contribute to the air the book has of the deliberate joke; but from then on, they play a much subtler part in the whole texture of the fantasy. They merge with the general underlying theme of the series: that the human thirst for romance and dignity is the cause of much disaster. When the Doctor is elected king of the Popsipetel people, in *The Voyages*, it is observed of him that he 'may not have been as dignified as many kings in history who were always running off and getting themselves into romantic situations'. Essentially, as one who is against war and fox-hunting and the romantic notions that accumulate around them, and as an opponent of riches and honours—as an obdurate non-conformist— Doctor Dolittle must be seen as a round, solid, sensible figure, without dash or conventional dignity. And the names, blunt as the Doctor's boots, are used to confirm the anti-romantic character of the tales and their meanings.*

The five books that followed *The Story*—*The Voyages of Doctor Dolittle* (1922), *Doctor Dolittle's Post Office* (1923), *Doctor Dolittle's Circus* (1924), *Doctor Dolittle's Zoo* (1925), and *Doctor Dolittle's Caravan* (1926)—form the ebullient, happy centre of the series. They follow no chronological sequence, but move about breathlessly among the events of the Doctor's life; and indeed they bear all the marks of Lofting's headlong delight in his own invention and in the world of fantastic creation to which it gave him entrance. It all seems to have come to him so fast that in his writing he is sometimes ahead of himself, sometimes behind. The

* In the later stories, when the fantasy is moving to a different and more delicate measure, these dumpy names sometimes work against the quality of Lofting's imagination. For the Moon Man, for example, described in *Doctor Dolittle's Return*—a romantic and gentle invention, touched with pathos— the name of Otho Bludge will not do. I remember a child who winced every time he came to it.

charming but thin air of the original joke has gone, and the arrival (in *The Voyages*) of Tommy Stubbins as narrator has given the Dolittle scene its new solidity. The invention of Stubbins was a beautiful stroke, for it not only enabled Lofting to tell the story from a boy's point of view (which carried the child reader, so to speak, into the story), but it added to the stature of Doctor Dolittle in young eyes by displaying the natural tact with which he himself approached children. Who could resist an adult who treated a boy of ten as a man, addressing him gravely as 'Stubbins'? Tommy is planted in the stories as the representative of many juvenile desires: not only to be so treated, but also, for example, to be seen off on a long voyage, as Stubbins is, by parents who behave well—that is, they do not make a scene. Now, with the reality of this world guaranteed by Stubbins' presence, Lofting can snatch out of the air those delicious imaginative audacities that, in *The Story*, merely seemed leg-pulls, but that henceforth will take on the colour of items from a scientific memoir. *The Voyages* is full of these. What made the island so inconveniently float? Because it was accidentally filled with air. How, then, for the sake of its inhabitants, to bring it to rest? Topple down a huge hanging stone, which will naturally pierce the air chamber and cause the island to settle to a carefully determined depth. How shall the imprisoned Long Arrow get a message to Doctor Dolittle? Of course, by tying an appeal for help to the leg of that rare Jabrizi beetle. Nothing would be more likely to catch the Doctor's eye. This happens; and Lofting follows the line of fantasy with patient attention until it leads him to Tommy Stubbins' pleasant comment: 'I had not realised before how hard it is for a human being to walk slowly enough to keep up with a beetle.' The whole tone is so unexcitable, so prosaic, that the stroke of imagination comes, time after time, as a marvellous surprise. Examples of this strange wedding of prosaic and poetic abound throughout the stories. A favourite with children is the journey home to Puddleby across the ocean floor in the great transparent snail (again in *The Voyages*). The discussion of this journey is so practical and hard-headed that the romantic oddity of it is immensely heightened.

But apart from these large ingenuities—such as the whole concept, at once breathtaking and down-to-earth, of the postal service conducted by birds in *Doctor Dolittle's Post Office*—there is an incessant flow of tiny curious detail to stir and delight a reader's imagination. Such details may be embodied in a phrase: as when that eloquent shellfish, the fidgit, begins its life story (listened to by the Doctor with his ear beneath the level of the water in the listening-tank): 'I was one of a family of two thousand five hundred and ten ...' Or as when Gub-Gub, the pig, telling his story about the Cook Goblins, mentions the 'cocoa-skin clothes lines' they invented—'little toy clothes lines to hang the skin off your cocoa on, neatly. (You know what a nasty mess it makes draped over the rim of your cup.)' The dogs' club, in *Doctor Dolittle's Zoo*, had 'a bone-rack (rather like an umbrella stand) ... provided for members near the front door'. Lofting's fertility, in the invention of such exquisite comic detail, never failed him, even after the early exuberance of the series had been left behind. It reaches its peak in the account of the Mooniversary Dinner in *Doctor Dolittle's Zoo*. Indeed, the entire description in this volume of the small animal societies set up by Doctor Dolittle in his garden, each with its own intricately worked out setting and mode of life, is a marvel of minutely detailed imaginative invention; but if anyone wanted a single example of the pure exhilaration that Lofting causes in a reader by this quality in his work, I would direct them to the Mooniversary Dinner—so called by the mice who arranged it because 'Anniversary means a year . . . A year's a long time in a mouse's life. [Let's] call it the Club's Mooniversary Dinner, to celebrate our month's birthday, not our year's birthday.'

'It was quite a novel sensation to be dining, shut up in a room into which we only just fitted, with five thousand rats and mice.
'At one of the upper doorways a small mouse orchestra played tunes throughout the dinner. Their instruments were invented by themselves and consisted of drums of different kinds and shapes and harps made by stretching threads across nutshells. One mouse had a straw which he played in the manner of a flute. Their idea of music was rather peculiar and very faint—indeed with the enormous chatter of squeaky conversation going on all around they could hardly be heard at all.'

To keep out the clatter of the washing-up, the door into the pantry is stopped up with a banana skin. It is a beautiful example of that combination of detailed veracity and general fantasy so characteristic of Lofting at his best.

After the Dinner, the Doctor amazes Stubbins by being able to recognise individual faces among the thousands of rats and mice around him. And, of course—amid all the curious inventions in these five books, the humour which ranges from the most ruthless punning to some subtle dry stroke of wit, thrown away—amid the plain excitements of voyaging, and the domestic comedies of the Doctor's household—there is deepening, always, the portrait of the Doctor himself as a man of uncommon sense and compassion, a nonconformist who goes to jail more often surely than any other hero of children's fiction, and with a greater sense that the prisoner may have more dignity than his jailer: as a man 'not fond of rules', who hates frauds, and publicity-seekers: as someone who so despises honours that he would prefer a pound of tea to a knighthood: as an opponent of all cruelty, but especially that of ordinary zoos, circuses and pet shops. The overgrown boy is left behind, and is replaced by someone of increasing moral stature—a critic of things as they are who creates instant and complete trust in those who meet him. The most obstinate difficulties give way before him: with no knowledge of sailing or navigation, he has only to take the helm of a ship to be sure of reaching his destination. He grows all the time, so that even his bachelorhood, based at first on a boyish joke, becomes a condition of his utter seriousness as a scientist: such a man, wrapped up in the quest for knowledge, filling an infinity of notebooks, would have no time for normal domestic life. 'When ever,' children have asked, 'did he have time to be a great gardener, too, and a great flautist?' But no young devotee of Doctor Dolittle ever complained that there was no rational answer to such questions. The greatness of the Doctor, as a creation, is that he is at once highly rational, and is not the prisoner of petty reason.

Perhaps none of the books of this period displays better than *Doctor Dolittle's Circus* that breathless zest and fantastic inventiveness of Lofting's writing which, more than anything else, accounts for the spell that the stories lay upon children who take to them. Quite apart from the account of the circus itself, of the Doctor's battle with the heartless conventions of circus life, and the ingenuity of the reforms he is able to bring about through his power to communicate with the animals, this volume, in which one episode treads fast on the heels of another, begins with the adventure in which the Doctor helps Sophie, the seal, to escape so that she can return to the sea and to her disconsolate husband, Slushy. Here is a typical Dolittle exploit, which starts from the notion that it is sheerly impossible. You simply cannot take a very large, slippery seal, whose element is the water, across a hundred miles of countryside to the sea. The idea is grotesque. Wonderfully—when, despite its impossibility, it *does* happen—it never ceases to be grotesque: John Dolittle's attempts to get Sophie up a ladder and over a wall into a garden, when they are desperately obliged to hide—or his attempt to travel with her in a stage coach, having disguised her as an old lady—: such enterprises remain quite absurd, comic nonsenses. And yet Lofting so handles them that, while remaining enormously funny, they inspire in a reader just the excitement that might be caused by reading the gravest of epics. It is something in his tone— and, even more, the irreducible gallantry of the Doctor himself—that enables Lofting, out of pure grotesque comedy, to extract pure serious excitement. But before the thrill of this is forgotten, we are plunged into an episode even more ridiculous, and even more guaranteed to make a young reader's pulses race. The Doctor finds himself in the middle of a fox hunt, and throws it into the most marvellous confusion by his power to talk sense both to the pursuing animals and their prey. One of the great moments in the Dolittle series comes when 'John Dolittle, *his pockets full of foxes*, ran out of the spinney after the Master of the Hunt'. As if such comic richness were not enough, the Doctor goes on to knock the bottom out of the fox-hunting world by handing round among the foxes his 'Dolittle Safety Packets' —concoctions of eucalyptus and camphor calculated to destroy the scent for the keenest of hounds.

Doctor Dolittle's Circus is, in my view, only by a rather special supercharge of high spirits and invention the best of these five books, which themselves form the happiest of all Lofting's writing. The stories that he wrote for the *Herald-*

Tribune and that posthumously were collected as *The Green Canary* and *The Puddleby Adventures* belong to the same confident period. But from then onwards a shadow falls. We know from Lofting's son Christopher that he had wearied of Dolittle; he 'tried to get rid of him by sending him to the Moon'. The attempt begins with *Doctor Dolittle's Garden*, published in 1927; a scrappy book, at first taking up the theme of *Doctor Dolittle's Zoo*, then turning to the Doctor's attempts to understand insect languages, and ending with his decision to go to the Moon. He has tired of 'the smaller geography':

' "Abroad!" John Dolittle's voice sounded to my surprise almost contemptuous. "Stubbins," he said suddenly in a strange, intense voice, "if I could get to the Moon!" '

His household is disturbed by the longings and dissatisfactions that have him in their thrall, and indeed the disturbance is felt by the reader. Mysteriously, the positive and determined John Dolittle has been replaced by an unhappy dreamer. It is clear enough that the change reflects a change in his creator. This was about the time of the sequence of tragedies in Lofting's own life—the death of his first wife, followed so soon by the death of his second. He had lived with John Dolittle for eight years and more, and had come, we must guess, to the end of the original impulse of delight that had carried him through all those books. But there seems also to have been a deepening of Lofting's pessimism about human affairs. 'The Moon,' says Polynesia, the parrot, 'is the only thing that would satisfy you—like a baby.' Little doubt that the Doctor's small taste for conventional human society reflected his maker's; to go to the Moon would be to escape that society even more thoroughly. Doctor Dolittle had at first held it against men that they sought riches and honours, were indifferent to the search for knowledge, were thoughtlessly cruel to animals. Now his criticism of the human scene grows more radical: the Dolittle of *The Story* is a long way from the Dolittle of the *Garden*, who says, neither simplifying the language nor softening the thought: 'It is the intuitive knowledge which we humans are so short on—especially the so-called civilised humans.'

The series had begun by way of revulsion from the inhumanity of the battlefield; and from the beginning it was possible to say that the Dolittle books were part of the anti-war literature that followed the Great War—a unique part of it, in being addressed to children. But the earlier stories were too exuberant to dwell with any bleakness on the tragedy of human wars. Now, in *Doctor Dolittle's Garden*, the theme breaks through in the wasp's story of his presence at a human battle:

'It seemed such a stupid waste. From one end of our beautiful valley armies would come with cannons and horses and everything . . . Then . . . they would go away again, leaving hundreds of dead men and horses on the ground which smelt horribly for a few days . . .'

By a typical stroke of ironic comedy, the wasp inadvertently changes the outcome of the battle; but the story remains the darkest of all those that, dotted throughout the books, usually so charmingly and lightly record the experiences of animals, insects, birds. (These inset stories form much of the miscellaneous material in the Dolittle books: many of them show the curious fantastic explicitness of Lofting's imagination at its best.) It is true that, here and there throughout the earlier adventures, Lofting has provided a political background to his world, in terms of the revolutionary befriended by a rat (*Doctor Dolittle's Zoo*), the machinery riots and the burning of a castle by revolted workers reported by Pippinella in her story (*The Green Canary*). A vague, warm-hearted, even sentimental radicalism has appeared at such moments, supporting his more precise attacks on human frailty with a view of the political world that saw it in terms of callous rulers, persecuted protesters. But until now, all this has had its setting of enormous general gaiety. There is still, of course, gaiety in *Doctor Dolittle's Garden*, and there is gaiety until the end: but now Lofting's anguished view of the conduct of living things comes through nakedly:

'This eternal war between the species—men against rats; rats against cats; cats against dogs, etc., etc., there is no end to it—must lead finally to some sort of tyranny ... What I would like to see ... would be a happy balance.'

The actual circumstances of the journey to the Moon, described in *Doctor Dolittle's Garden*, are treated with all of Lofting's lively ingenuity. The scene of the arrival of the great moth that has come to fetch the Doctor on his medical errand (he is needed to tend to the ailing Moon Man) is one not easily forgotten, either for its grotesque poetry or for the characteristic measures taken by John Dolittle to revive the exhausted creature.

'He worried Dab-Dab to death by buying oil stoves by the dozen to set around the garden and supplemented these by hot water bottles actually in hundreds.'

The journey itself, with the travellers using the bells of huge moon flowers as oxygen masks, is like science fiction rewritten in terms of a queer poetic comedy. And there are many curious, typical and unforgettable touches in the stay on the moon, such as the episode when, finding the vanity lilies dying because the pools in which they admired themselves had dried up, the Doctor (with the help of his bottomless travelling bag) provides them with makeshift mirrors. But, though the detail retains this imaginative quaintness that has become Dolittle's hallmark, the atmosphere is twilit: the full day of the earlier stories has gone. The Moon is a utopia that strengthens the Doctor's growing pessimism about life on earth. There, on the planet, there was no struggle between the animal and vegetable kingdoms: 'We found the whole system of life . . . a singularly peaceful business.' John Dolittle reflects sadly: 'With us it is, and always has been, "dog eats dog" '; and as he trudges about the mysterious surface of the Moon, there is something suddenly forlorn and desolate about the chubby, sensible little man, as described and illustrated. It is as if a character from comedy, though a thoughtful and altogether unusual character, had suddenly wandered into the atmosphere of tragedy. When he comes to describe the Moon, he says, 'I find myself wishing that I were a great poet, or at all events a great writer. For this moon-world was indeed a land of wondrous rest . . .'

This, Christopher Lofting tells us, was to be Doctor Dolittle's Reichenbach Falls. Here he was to remain, ministering to the Moon Man and filling his everlasting notebooks, while his friends on earth waited for his return, hopefully, for ever. But the resurrection of his hero was demanded of Lofting, as it was of Conan Doyle. *Doctor Dolittle's Return* again has its typical excitements and imaginative audacities. What child (as I know from reading these books with many children) ever forgets the arrival of the Doctor on earth, grown enormous by moon chemistry, and being for a long time unable to enter his own house! There are still delightful jokes—jokes that are pure Lofting:

'People on the earth, you know, have always spoken of *The Man in the Moon*, but I hope that when my book is written—and read—they will come to speak of the *Gentleman in the Moon*.' The Doctor's capacity for curious reasoning is unimpaired, as when he explains why there is no vegetable language on earth; hybridisation, he suggests, has brought about a situation in which 'the poor thing doesn't even know whether he's a raspberry or a rose'. But John Dolittle has returned to earth more, not less, anxious about the future of life here.

'Anyone who studies natural history must come to fear sooner or later that all life faces a losing game down here with us . . . Life keeps on killing life. The fly is swallowed by the fish; the fish is eaten by the duck; the duck is devoured by the fox; the fox is slaughtered by the wolf; the wolf is shot by the man, and then men—the only ones on top in our world—turn round and kill one another in war.'

For once, though he never loses their loyalty, he has exhausted the patience of his household. There is affection, but there is also something careworn, about his housekeeper Dab-dab's outcry against his perpetual concern for more and more minute living creatures: 'He'll have a Wardrobe for clothing Moths or a Bedroom for Bedbugs before you know where you are.' But the strongest sign that Lofting was now building into the stories his sense that his longing for peace, expressed through John Dolittle, had become rather dark and desperate and obsessive, lies perhaps in Polynesia's reaction to another of these speeches (so rarely long for Doctor Dolittle) that he makes on his return to earth. The Doctor says:

'. . . You can all very well see, can't you? that when I found a world which was run along sensible lines, where no kind of life trod on the toes of any other kind of life, I began to wonder if something of those ideas could be brought home and started here.'

Polynesia's response is simply to swear, in Swedish. It is partly a joke—Polynesia has always been a sensible, as well as a polyglot, bird; but it also seems to embody a very real gesture of self-deprecation on Lofting's part.

It is not my suggestion that, with these later books, the heart has gone out of the Dolittle series. Far from it. There are shadows, now, over the Dolittle world, and what for so long was so bubbling and gay is now shot through with melancholy. This is part of the total experience that this remarkable series gives to its readers: for some children, it may be the most influential and memorable part. But the author's personal misfortunes, his poor health, the approach of the 1930s with the dying hope they brought of international sanity, made him feed into his stories an exhaustion that is expressed through the Doctor himself, and a concerned bewilderment which becomes, in these books that revolve round the journey to the Moon, the mood of the Doctor's little household. They watch over him now, worriedly. ' "There he is," whispered Matthew, "workin' away. Ain't it like 'im?—Tryin' to set the world to rights?" ' And the Doctor himself, for the first time, is simply worried:

' "All my life I've never had time enough . . . The older we grow the more worried we get. Worried! Worried that we won't get what we want done." '

It is clearly the Doctor's creator who speaks. But his skill enables him to make comedy even out of such melancholy. For now, wishing to write his great book about the Moon, the Doctor is prevented from working by the queues of animals waiting to be doctored—longer than ever after his absence. So his household hit upon the neat idea that, in order to gain the solitude he needs, he should contrive to go to jail. At once, dispelling the sadness that has accumulated, Lofting's gift for farce takes over, and there follow episodes in quite the old style: his tuition in simple crime by that old jailbird, Matthew Mugg; the comic setback he suffers when he breaks the window of a house and is balked of his proper punishment by Lady Matilda Beamish, an admirer of the great man, who is only too delighted to pay his fine; and the ultimate comedy of his rescue from jail, when he at last contrives to be sent there, by his friends the rodents, who cannot conceive that he should not wish to be rescued. It is the old gaiety, in the end, that sets the seal on this, fundamentally, sad trio of books.

The final volume, *Doctor Dolittle and the Secret Lake*, took thirteen years in the writing, and is a book that falls curiously into two halves. The first half is full of the familiar enchantments: the beginning in the Puddleby household, the decision to take yet another journey, the journey itself. The Doctor is still low-spirited; he has been working, with the moon seeds he brought back with him to earth, on the secret of everlasting life. As he explained to Stubbins, now his fully-trained secretary, 'the trouble with our world down here was *time*. People were in such a hurry. If, said he, Man knew he could live as long as he wanted, then he would stop all this crazy rushing around; this fear—which even he, the easygoing John Dolittle, had felt—would be taken from us . . . Yes, it was a great dream.' But now he has given up that dream—he is beaten. Polynesia is impatient. 'He's gone stale,' she says. 'He needs a change from this beastly English climate.' It is, in some senses, the familiar formula for starting a Dolittle adventure: boredom sets in, the whole household needs a change: someone, as if it had never happened before, wistfully suggests that they might go travelling; and, by the operation of a most satisfactory magic, at once the opportunity for adventure arises. In this case they hear that Mudface, the ancient turtle, has disappeared from the African lake that is his home. Long ago, in *Doctor Dolittle's Post Office*, the making of an island where Mudface might live had been one of the most memorable fantastic scenes in the series: the island was built by millions of birds dropping, first pebbles and gravel, and then sand, and finally grass and other seeds, into the lake. Now, in this new adventure, a rescue operation is called for, and is the more eagerly embarked on by the Doctor because Mudface is a survivor of the Flood; and that is a story that has still to be recorded in the notebooks.

The theme, then, is worthy of a last book. This will be John Dolittle's greatest scientific exploit; it will be led up to by an adventure of rescue; it will raise his spirits, never so low. And indeed, the old energy of invention is at work throughout the whole of this first half of the story. The comic interplay of character among his travelling companions was never more lively. (It is in this book that Cheapside, the Cockney sparrow, describes Polynesia as 'a flying dishrag', and Dab-Dab, the patient housekeeper, expresses her horror at finding the white mouse bunked down aboard ship in a teacup: 'Mice in *my* chinarack!') And Lofting has lost none of his power to create a sudden warm fantastic scene, which makes young readers shiver with delight at an imaginative opportunity seized; as when, on its arrival at Fantippo, the ship is boarded by so many visitors ('like ants on a jam-pot') that it nearly sinks. And from now on, until the rescue of Mudface, he keeps, as so often in the stories, a small throb of constant excitement going, with its climax in one of the very best of his big, heroic, preposterous scenes. Mudface, they discover, is buried at the bottom of the lake in the ruins of his island. The only way to rescue him is to call upon the crocodiles and get them to dig the turtle out. And they come in multitudes:

'The right bank of the river rose here to quite a height. And down this slope the crocodiles from the Niger were pouring—in a solid procession—into the Little Fantippo River. The jungle, whose heavy tangle covered all the land on either bank, had here been torn up and cleaned off by millions of clawed feet, making a wide, crowded road.

'You could barely see the ground they walked on—only the creatures' backs, as close together as stitches in a carpet. But once in a while a free spot in the parade would open up; and then you saw that the earth had been trodden as smooth as a pavement.'

Then follows the rescue and—it is to be the climax of the whole series—the recording of Mudface's memories of the Flood.

No story, clearly, could have served Lofting's purpose better, at the end (and he must have felt that it was the end) of the series. He handles it typically—a mixture of the queerly practical and the imaginative—and gives the legend a twist of his own, Mudface and his wife saving the lives of two humans and so assuring for mankind another chance. The whole Dolittle saga is given an extra depth when Mudface discloses that Noah, too, was a speaker of animal languages; suddenly, at this point, we see the Doctor as a re-created Noah, and this comic myth is brushed by a greater one. Yet for a second time, it seems to me, the Dolittle magic proves defective. The first time was on the Moon when, for all the characteristic and endearing ingenuity of the narrative, the poetic elements in the story were at times in conflict with the essential nature of the Dolittle series, which is one of broad humour and even burlesque. And now, once again, Lofting takes his little company into what is truly a world of poetry, and the honest prose he employs does not quite carry him through.

The point is a difficult one, and I am brought to it not only by my own readings of *The Secret Lake*, but also by the common response of children to the second half of it: which is to find it curiously dull. It seems to me that in fact the concept of the series, its hilarities, its deadpan exaggerations, prevent it from ever rising to the heights to which, in these last books, but especially in the second half of *The Secret Lake*, Lofting was trying to take it. The concept had been able to support so many of his underlying seriousnesses, and even in the three books concerned with the voyage to the Moon, swept through though they are with a growing despair about the future of life on earth, the solid, touching image of the Doctor had almost held its own. But when we come to the story of the Flood, even Mudface's name sets up a conflict between itself and the imaginative atmosphere of the story. The events of the Flood have, in many respects, the tone of a typical Dolittle adventure; they are full of blunt, characteristically inelegant detail. Even the impatient interjections of the Doctor's companions, as the old turtle slowly tells his tale, seem at odds with the tale itself—or rather, with the high legend lurking behind it.

All this is merely to say that, in my opinion, and by the highest standards I am able to apply, the second half of *The Secret Lake* is a failure. It is so because, in the last analysis, the Dolittle stories by their nature cannot deal with legendary material so reverberant with poetry. In a sense, from *The Garden* onwards Lofting had been trying to make the series carry graver implications than, for all its quality, it was made to carry. Yet, having said this, one must add that the failure is a noble one: perhaps nobody else has ever tried, through a literary conception constructed to amuse and delight children, to say as much as these last books were attempting to say. And for all the strain that is set up between the essential limitations of the series, and the vision the author was attempting to pour into it, no one—and certainly no child—is ever the worse for having seen the Moon through Doctor Dolittle's eyes, or having read or listened to Mudface's curious account of the Flood. By another critic it might well be maintained that the prosy nature of that account—its being turned, as it were, into a special sort of Dolittle adventure—is thoroughly justified, since there is nothing sacred about the legend and it cannot be anything but good to retell it in terms entertaining to children. I could not agree with this view—and largely because I have found that children are not entertained by the story as Lofting told it: but this is certainly arguable.

I have had to devote so much attention to the second half of *The Secret Lake* because I believe that one of the most interesting qualities of the Dolittle series, to any critic, must be the way Lofting made it say so much, and built so high upon an idea that was basically a broadly comic and stubbornly anti-romantic one: it is therefore important for a critic to mark the point where, as he sees it, the building grew a little higher than its foundations could bear. But, as would be agreed by most of the children I know who have made their way through the whole series, the Doctor himself loses nothing by this failure of the final tale to reproduce the magic of so many of those that went before it. It is a long way from the giggling bachelor of *The Story*; but, perhaps because Lofting put so much of himself into the character, it is still the same Doctor Dolittle—the same preoccupied, sensible, compassionate man—who promises Mudface, when his story is told, that he will write it all down in a book. If he does that, says Mudface, 'maybe war may stop altogether'.

'The Doctor, silent, thought a moment before he answered.

' "Indeed, I hope so," he sighed at last. "At least I promise you the book shall be written and I will do my best to write it well. How many will take any notice of it: that is another matter. For men are deaf, mind you, Mudface—deaf when they do not wish to hear and to remember—and deafest of all when their close danger is ended with a short peace, and they *want* to believe that war will not come back." '*

'He sighed': and the sighing John Dolittle—the sighing Hugh Lofting—is part of the unique image we carry away from these books. But there is also a laughing John Dolittle, and of course a laughing Hugh Lofting; and it is with them that this last of the long, marvellous series comes to an end. As the Doctor's family bid farewell to Mudface and Belinda, his wife, Polynesia can be heard singing alone:

> ' "For she's a jolly good fellow.
> Yes, she's a jolly good fell-Hello!
> Oh, Belinda's a jolly good fell-Hello!"

'The Doctor and I broke into outright laughter. For the parrot had set the words to the tune of a sailor's hornpipe.

'Then, like one man with one thought, John Dolittle and I plunged our paddles into the starlit water at the same moment. The canoe shot forward into the river like an arrow (upsetting most of the merry-makers in a laughing heap on top of the baggage). We were on our way downstream, towards the West, towards Puddleby and home.'

* The tone, one notes, is closer to plain preaching than anywhere else in the Dolittle books; and part of one's uneasiness about *The Secret Lake* may be due to this naked earnestness that emerges in it.

III. Other Works

It is a pity that, overshadowed by the Dolittle books, most of Lofting's other work has been so long out of print. To each of his various gifts as a writer, the Dolittle series acted at the same time as a stimulus and a limitation. His sense of utterly happy comic fun, for example, permeates these books; but to enjoy it in its pure form, one needs to read *Gub Gub's Book*, which appeared in 1932. Again, the Dolittle books deal in nothing if not in magic; but since the Doctor was a scientist, the magic had to be of a practical kind; and to discover what Lofting could do with traditional, inexplicable magic, one must turn to *The Twilight of Magic* (1930). In each of his incidental writings, a part of Lofting's talent is seen in its absolute form; and this is always a delight.

The first of the non-Dolittle books appeared in 1923: *The Story of Mrs Tubbs*, a picture book for the very young. The story is charming and characteristic. Mrs Tubbs, one hundred years old, is driven from her home by a hard-hearted landlord. She is befriended by a dog, a duck and a pig, who set out to recover her home by making the landlord's life thoroughly miserable. They summon to their aid the rats, but these are routed by the landlord's cats; then the swallows, under their queen, Tilly Twitter, but they too are driven off. Victory comes when they mobilise the wasps. Amid all this, Mrs Tubbs is merely a silent sufferer, a mute cause of the busy ingenious kindliness of the animals. Her silence haunts the story, beautifully. The illustrations are unlike any others that Lofting drew, of enchanting simplicity and tenderness. Mrs Tubbs is caught exactly, a round

speechless old lady with a puzzled blob of a face, and she
and the animals exist in a world usually reduced to a typical
Lofting tree or two, pastel-shaded. One vignette, 'They all
walked back to the farm by moonlight', shows Mrs Tubbs
and her companions trudging in silhouette past a scattering
of poplars and under a big simple moon; and it has, as the
whole story has, the haunting, dream-like simplicity of the
very best picture books for the young. A sequel, *Tommy,
Tilly and Mrs Tubbs*, was published in 1937, and has much
the same theme; this time the old lady's house is blown down
in a storm, and her animal friends take her to the woods,
where the swallows make her a house of leaves. In a rough
wind this is blown away—'three wagon-loads of leaves
flew, swirling, through the forest, scattered and disappeared'. (The precision as to the quantity of leaves is
pure Lofting.) Two children are called upon to repair
Mrs Tubbs' original house, and the season of terrible winds
comes to a happy end. These are slight books, but only in
the sense that all picture books for very young children are
slight; in fact, they carry in a simple, moving form Lofting's
invariable messages: the importance of kindness, the need to
construct rather than destroy.

In 1925 the comic poet in him had an airing in *Porridge
Poetry*, 'Cooked, Ornamented and Served Up by Hugh
Lofting'. The frontispiece is characteristic, showing the
author at work in his poetic kitchen, surrounded by jars
marked 'Dried Pronouns' and 'Syrup of Verbs' and a
pepper pot labelled 'Syntax'. One day, perhaps, someone
will be able to explain the stress in all Lofting's writing on
the pleasures of food; it is certainly one of the reasons why
the stories delight children so much. (The esurient Gub Gub
is a child's hero, if ever there was one.) 'As for comic songs
or ballads,' Lofting writes, 'I turn them out like summer

salads'; and some of them are very comic indeed. Many rest
on his tireless, Ogden Nash-like playfulness with words:

> 'Twas in the tropic latitudes
> That we were talking platitudes,
> Just sailor-like chit-chatitudes,
>   As any ship-mates might.

> We forgot to take our longitude
> (Which was a grievous wrongitude)
> So we didn't reach Hong-Kongitude
>   Till very late that night.

Others suggest nothing so much as Cautionary Verses by
Hilaire Belloc ferociously abbreviated by Lewis Carroll and
Edward Lear, working together: as in the case of 'Scrubby
Chubby', a poem that, facing an illustration of a hideously
unhappy child holding a broken toy horse, merely com-
ments:

Such a scowling and a growling, howling yowling for a toy,
You grubby, snubby, tubby, chubby, scrubby little boy!

These poems fall into the tradition of English nonsense
verse, and Lofting is a minor figure in the field; but the best
of them are gay accessions to it, and the whole book in its
original form—an agreeable oblong, the letters of the title
made out of posturing piemen and tophatted gentlemen and
maidservants—is so evocative of its period that it deserves
reprinting.

   This is true also of *Noisy Nora*, a cautionary tale in prose
published in 1929 and printed in Lofting's own lettering.
This is nothing more than the salutary story of a little girl
who was, and insisted on remaining, a noisy eater. She is
exiled to the kitchen of the farm where she lives, but the
farm hands and dairy maids refuse to endure the noise of

her eating; so she is sent to the stable, where the horses complain; and so to the cowsheds and the pigsties. When she is relegated to an empty barn, the rats protest. So at last she is made to take her meals in a fenced enclosure in the open fields, but the very birds flee. The worms seize this chance to emerge, but they too, appalled, are forced to retreat. In the 'great calm silence' that fell, the noise of Nora's eating 'jarred and disgusted even herself', and she became a reformed character. Just as one wishes Lofting had spared more time for nonsense verse, so one regrets that he did not write more in this vein. Traditionally, the cautionary tale for children has an horrific edge; to it, in *Noisy Nora*, Lofting brought his own highly individual quality of gentle ingenuity.

The Twilight of Magic appeared in 1930; without lacking many of the typical features of Lofting's narratives—the curious detail and the inventive surprises—it is the story in which he came closest to the romantic world of the fairy tale. In it, he let go for once of those blunt elements in his writing, the obstinate homeliness of humour and the broadly comic naming of characters, that elsewhere represented his refusal to abandon himself to romance. Plainly, romance seemed to him dangerous because it had so often served to give glamour to human activities and attitudes he detested, and especially the activity of war. But in *The Twilight of Magic* he rested his story on magic pure and unexplained, and this seems to have been an enfranchisement. Giles and his sister Anne, inhabiting some characteristically vague country and moment of history, acquire a magic seashell; whoever listens to it is able to hear whatever is being said about him, anywhere. They use it to save the life of the young king of their country. Deeply written into the story, under the lucid and charming surface of the narrative, are many of

Lofting's major themes: that children are likely to have clearer and truer vision than adults: that happiness is impossible without trust: that war is no solution of human problems. There is a moment, curious in the whole context of Lofting's work, when the king, anxious to reward Giles, turns to the boy and asks for his family name. Giles replies that it is 'Waggonwright'; and the king comments:

' "Waggonwright—No. I don't like that so well. But never mind. It has an honest sound." '

Compared with the comically honest sound of the names of most of Lofting's characters, 'Waggonwright' is almost elegant; and the king seems to be expressing, as it were, something of the author's own astonishment, that he can build a world in which the young hero is called Giles, and the king's own horses are beautifully named Africa and Midnight, and yet, romantic though this all is, the world is still Lofting's, and one in which traditional magic and blunt reason can live together. And in a sense, it is the wedding of these two qualities that had eluded Lofting in the final volumes of the Dolittle saga, simply because the broadly comic basis of the Dolittle books prevented Lofting from bringing about such a delicate balance between romance and common sense as is found in *The Twilight of Magic*.

It is odd that *Gub Gub's Book*, which appeared in 1932, should not be regarded without question as a part of the Dolittle canon. True, the Doctor does not appear in it; but this is the first and only volume of that twenty-volume Encyclopaedia of Food referred to frequently in conversation in the Dolittle household, and in it a joyously free rein is given to one of the richest of the jests that thread their way through the Dolittle books. This is the jest of gluttony, and *Gub Gub's Book* is a breathlessly funny elaboration of it.

At one moment Gub Gub is proposing that railway time-tables might be converted into bills-of-fare, so that you would go to a booking office and say: 'I want a ticket to the best pudding you have'; at another he is suggesting that Shakespeare be rewritten so as to encourage serious reading among young pigs ('Lay on, Plumduff! and burst be he who first can't hold enough!'). Other members of the household make their contributions, as when the White Mouse recalls that he was once 'pea-fielder' for a little boy whose 'peas spilled and ran all over the place'. It is a world of outrageous jokes. Lemonade poured into a river changes the speckled trout in it into 'the far-famed *sour-faced* trout'. A journalist called Hamilton Sandwich is, of course, known to his friends as 'Ham Sandwich'. Gub Gub's projected novel is 'an Epicnic'. And even here, in the midst of this high-spirited nonsense, Lofting says the serious things that he believed it was so important to say to children. Gub Gub tells the story of the War of the Tomatoes, in which tomatoes formed the only ammunition; and this leads Cheapside the sparrow to comment:

' "A very juicy bit of 'istry, Perfesser—still, if you must 'ave wars I reckon that's as good a kind as any. From what I can make out, there ain't been none of 'em what's brought much more profit to either side, than that—just a valley full of ketchup." '

To which, using comedy as a means of curiously deepening a serious comment, as he knew so well how to do, Lofting makes Gub Gub reply:

' "Ah, but the loss in vegetable stuff! All those tomatoes! A race wiped out! Terrible, terrible!" '

The last of these writings of Lofting's that one must, in the shadow of the Dolittle books, describe as incidental, was not for children; it was the bitterest thing he ever wrote, a poem called *Victory for the Slain* that was published in 1942. Lofting cannot be taken seriously as a poet (other than a comic one), but the passionate despair that marked the end of his life, and that lay its shadow on the character of John Dolittle himself, is here seen in most moving nakedness. The poet, out walking, sees

> a soldier all alone
> Here seated on the High Street's curb of stone.
> The blue of hospital he wears.
> Around his feet lie matches' embers.
> If we forget he still remembers.
> His features pale show no regret;
> But with his mates—and thousands yet,
> Can he forget?

Thinking that 'in war the only victors are the slain', the poet walks on and enters a church. Even here he is reminded of battle by the tattered banners and standards that hang on the walls. The sight of the poor box reminds him of the malign power of money:

> What has money, in its essence
> Or as an instrument of power, consigned us?
> To hoard is not to earn—
> Money-power in Past, as now,
> Made continents in devastation burn.

In his head he hears the marching of feet, and cannot tell one army from another—that of his own war, that of the new one:

> It's every score of years and five
> That they return.

He imagines war following war, in a fearful sequence:

> When nation against nation
> Shall at last lay down their arms,
> Will class against another come—
> The Reds against the Whites?
> And faiths and races, too . . . ?

The poem ends with a scream—the poet's, and that of a bomb falling from an aeroplane overhead:

> At last, with whistling scream, it strikes.
> Cutting through the chancel-roof like paper,
> The bomb
> Explodes before the tabernacle of our dreams.

Against the scream he sets a tiny hope, symbolised by a small door in one wall of the church: such a door must remain for Man as

> His ultimate escape
> From this returning curse,
> His malady of mind . . .

Reading *Victory for the Slain*, a poem of pure anguish: and remembering that behind it lies the long, high-spirited, inventive saga of John Dolittle, that gentle comedy for children through which Hugh Lofting sought to give them a vision of man's most serious problems; doing this, one is bound to think of Doctor Dolittle himself, in his last phase, weary and saddened, and to feel the profoundest compassion for a writer who, working for so long with such hope, came at the end of his own days to such desolate hopelessness.

> Planes!—Planes over playgrounds,
> Over prayers for the dead—the freshly dead!
> Useless! . . . Uselessness!

IV. The Illustrator

Although he had illustrated those letters to his children that he sent home from France, and had in fact been trained as a civil engineer with an architectural bias, it appears that Lofting did not at first think of illustrating his own work when it was published. He belongs, indeed, to that small and precious class of author-illustrators whose drawing, by any ordinary judgement, was barely competent. To the end, John Dolittle's arms appeared to be attached to his torso by some entirely novel means. But an important part of the spell cast by the Dolittle books is owed to the illustrations, and we must be grateful that his first publishers were able to recognise their unconventional charm, and did not replace what had been meant as helpful sketches with the work of a professional illustrator.

It is, in *The Story of Doctor Dolittle*, scarcely charm. The influences at work on Lofting's early style as an illustrator are difficult to track down; I suspect myself that he may have been feeling for the sort of comic image that was expressed in the figures that writhed and cavorted round the original cover of *Punch*. These early drawings have an elaborate grotesquerie that offers us a John Dolittle of almost forbidding ugliness. In the frontispiece to *The Story* he resembles the apes that surround him. Black-eyed, formidably eyebrowed, he is not yet Doctor Dolittle at all, in any recognisable sense. He is a comic monster, and is surrounded by others. This is indeed the world of early Victorian slapstick and satire, in which ugliness itself is taken to be comic. The Africans come out of it worst, and

Bumpo the worst of the Africans; the broad tip of the Negro nose is broadened until it stretches from side to side of the prince's face. Sarah Dolittle certainly never recovers from that first image we have of her, hideous, square, enraged. Yet already the essence of the Dolittle world is established. The interiors are as they were to remain—oblongs filled with homely graceless tables and chairs: the eternal kitchens of an ideal childhood, where nothing can be harmed, being decrepit already. Lofting's lack of the professional artist's skill enabled him also, even in this untypically over-elaborate early period, to make curiously attractive simple statements in his drawing. If Bumpo is in bed, for example, then we have a bed, foursquare and uncompromisingly non-African, in an otherwise bare room, with one of Lofting's moons staring through the simple square of the window. From the beginning he draws trees and mountains as though they had personalities. His favourite tree is squat and twisted (its branches much-used to give a drawing a sort of pokerwork frame), and seems about to speak, or to take part in the action. But what, in these early drawings, connects us most closely with the illustrations to come is Lofting's way with animals. Except where seen in close-up (when Lofting is more ambitious) they have simple outlines, which scarcely ever varied throughout the series. A dog, a pig, a duck in *The Story* are already as they were to remain: curiously touching little ideographs. In some of the interiors they are to be tracked down, in the shadows, watching over the scene.

As with the style of the text, so with the style of the illustrations—by the second book already the change has begun. The Doctor has ceased to be a monster, and has been reduced to the benign simplicity of the final image. He is Tommy Stubbins' 'funny little man' with a 'kind, smiling face . . . comfortable, sensible, friendly and solid'. The snub nose, the mouth oddly often down-turned (we have to take the smile on trust, as often as not), two dots for eyes, the flat head and practical haircut: that is, and ever will be John Dolittle. It is impossible to tell how conscious Lofting was of his technique as an illustrator; but certainly he had a gift, employed at its very best in the middle books of the series, for varying a closeup with a distant scene, for scribbling some simple pictorial statement and then following it with something most enjoyably elaborate. We are rarely left unaware, in any lengthy episode, of the total character of a scene—we have whole islands, a complete and oppressive view of a prison cell, and Puddleby itself is made thoroughly familiar to us: a largely empty toy town, with ships of an uncertain period tied up at the quay and, like all Lofting's ships, rather standing upon the water than immersed in it.

It seems to me that, as the series developed, two important things happened to Lofting as illustrator. The first was that he was able to feed into his illustrations more and more of the growing gentleness and mystery of the narrative; the conscious ugliness disappears, the world within those hand-drawn frames reflects more and more of the wistful, comic, practical poetry of the Dolittle scene. Second, he learned to reduce what he had to say, pictorially, to a minimum of quick lines, so that by the time we reach *Doctor Dolittle in the Moon* the illustrations delight by their pure economy. They come to resemble, as it were, comic Japanese prints. The evocative scribbles that represent the events on the Moon are followed, in *Doctor Dolittle and the Secret Lake*, by a return to greater deliberation; but, fed by the long experience of those hundreds of drawings, it is an economical deliberation.

As an illustrator, as in so many other respects, Lofting

was an original. It is possible to guess at the styles of drawing that influenced him—a curious range from early Victorian grotesquerie to art nouveau—and the general character of the illustrations ties the books very firmly to the 1920s. Yet in essence his manner is his own, unique and unmistakable, and his texts would lose much of their quality if those curious, beautifully awkward and entirely suitable illustrations were ever removed from them.

v. A Summing Up

I have said before in this study that Hugh Lofting was an original, and it seems to me quite the most important thing to say about him. His originality lies in none of his specific talents. His sense of comedy, punning and often facetious, or depending on a startling alliance of the preposterous and the practical, is not unique. The early books especially bear strong marks of their period, in a certain cosiness, a sense that adventures properly end with feasts of bread and butter and strawberry jam. Anyone making a collection of children's books that were redolent of the 1920s would be bound to choose the Dolittles. And yet Lofting's work stands alone, among writing for children, for one very important reason. It is not the only children's fiction that has behind it a conscious purpose that might, in the widest sense, be called political. But no one else has set out, quite as he did, to create a hero, and a notion of heroism, that is radical, pacifist and profoundly opposed to common ideas of conventional respectability. The rich fun of the Dolittle stories and their marvellous and enduring novelty tend to obscure from us their deeply nonconformist nature. There is no means of calculating the effect they have had on children who have read them. One can only guess with some confidence that, having once identified yourself with John Dolittle, you would thereafter find it more difficult to identify yourself with the world's anti-Dolittles; with those who are cruel, and not only to animals, and with those who seek after riches and honours.

The stories have from time to time been discussed as

though they were primarily a part of that children's literature that is concerned with talking animals. Hugh Walpole looked at *The Story of Doctor Dolittle* in this light. It seems to me that, though the essence of the stories may seem to be that they are about animals that talk, the books are really about human behaviour. It is not merely the author's remarkable powers of persuasion that make us forget, much of the time, that we are moving among animals.* It is also that the conduct and talk of his creatures is so often made to reflect on the ways of men and women. One can carry this argument too far, and obviously part of the charm and delight of the Dolittle books lies in their feeling for animal identity; but surely in a wider sense we are in the atmosphere of a metaphor, and when our attention seems to be directed to some oddity of animal existence, it is really some oddity of human existence that is being illuminated. In a sense, Lofting used animals to underline the unsatisfactory nature of the human world. When he says that 'the animal sense of humour is far superior to the human', he is giving us a salutary dig. And Polynesia, when she remarks: 'I suppose if people ever learn to fly—like any common hedgesparrow—we shall never hear the end of it', is being used to make Lofting's young readers reflect on the absurdity of human pride and pretensions.

It is even possible to say that a healthy young reader ought, at some point, to quarrel with Doctor Dolittle, and with his desertion of the world of human medicine. Lofting said that the Doctor turned away from 'the mere human hypochondriac', and those humans who seek the help of medicine are, of course, not all hypochondriacs, by any means. At the roots of this unique fantasy lies a pessimism

* I remember a child who said to me once: 'I just can't remember that Polynesia is a *parrot*. She keeps reminding me of Mrs ——' (naming a neighbour).

about the world of men that a child should detect and question. There can be little doubt that Lofting would have been delighted if they did so. His aim was always to be provocative.

For a long time Doctor Dolittle has been a special taste among children, if only because really to enter and inhabit his world requires some literary patience and endurance. The books have been translated into many languages, and today they seem on the brink of a new and wider life, appearing as paperbacks (in a Puffin edition) and forming the basis of a film. It is difficult to compare them with other children's classics, since they are so much more diffuse— simply, so much longer, when put together. But if the appetite for series, when they first appeared, was largely confined to the literate households of the time, it is now a taste much more widely spread, and one hopes that the new chapter in their history will bring them an immense new audience.

One hopes this especially because the world is still racked with those hatreds that in his writing, and in his choosing to write for children, Lofting hoped to play a part in dispelling. His work will always be rewarding for that richly inventive playfulness that is the mark of it—for the pure fun and surprise that it offers its readers, largely but not all young ones. Yet it is never possible to forget, in enjoying the high spirits of this writing at its best, that it stands high above most other writing for children for having at its heart this profound concern for sane behaviour among living creatures. And it immeasurably strengthens rather than weakens this humaneness of purpose that Lofting so often expressed it in terms utterly suitable for his audience, gay and light: as when (one really should end on Lofting's own special note of comic seriousness) the Doctor restricts his conversation with the twenty-four hour greenfly on the grounds that, for him, a half an hour of talking is the equivalent of eighteen months of a human life. It is really in the accumulation of such small comic touches, so many of them expressing most lightly a most serious concern with gentleness and kindness, that the importance of Hugh Lofting's work for children lies.

BIBLIOGRAPHY

Bibliography

(*All Hugh Lofting's work has been published in Great Britain by Jonathan Cape Ltd*)

The Story of Doctor Dolittle, 1920
The Voyages of Doctor Dolittle, 1922
Doctor Dolittle's Post Office, 1923
The Story of Mrs Tubbs, 1923
Doctor Dolittle's Circus, 1924
Porridge Poetry, 1925
Doctor Dolittle's Zoo, 1925
Doctor Dolittle's Caravan, 1926
Doctor Dolittle's Garden, 1927
Doctor Dolittle in the Moon, 1929
Noisy Nora, 1929
The Twilight of Magic, 1930
Gub Gub's Book, 1932
Doctor Dolittle's Return, 1933
Tommy, Tilly and Mrs Tubbs, 1937
Victory for the Slain, 1942
Doctor Dolittle and the Secret Lake, 1949
Doctor Dolittle and the Green Canary, 1950
Doctor Dolittle's Puddleby Adventures, 1952

Geoffrey Trease

MARGARET MEEK

For
IAN MICHAEL
and the students at the
Royal Fort

CONTENTS

I Introduction, 67

II Early Work, 77

III The Historical Adventure Story, 86

IV *Tales out of School*, 101

V 'Children just like us', 104

VI Travel Fiction, 119

VII Methods and Translations, 121

VIII Conclusion, 125

Bibliography, 129

E

1. Introduction

Nothing is so characteristic of the English as the way they take important things for granted. Children's reading is a matter of some concern at the present time, and it is fashionable to say that children no longer get the pleasure from reading that their parents did, although hundreds of new titles appear every year, every good bookshop is full of excellent examples of story-telling and the writer's craft, and since the second World War there has been a publishers' revolution. What is rarely admitted is that when some of the authors, so highly praised by parents in their fifties, were in full spate, the majority of English children were barking at print in elementary school primers. These were the books specially written for children to teach them to read, or to give them their first experience in reading, but they gave no indication that the proper pleasure of reading was other than the relief of word recognition.

So many things have changed in the production of children's books in this century that it is difficult in a series of Monographs which deals chiefly with his distinguished predecessors to set in perspective a contemporary writer who has worked unremittingly for the cause of children's literature. We should do the work of Geoffrey Trease less than justice if we thought that he had a broad highway before him when he left Oxford in 1929 and went to London to seek his fortune as a writer. Nor could he then have been attracted to writing for children. This was the period of the Bumper Books, those swollen puffboard monstrosities printed on featherweight paper and judged by their bulk.

The influence of the hack writer was at its height. No wonder, then, that those who wanted suitable books for their young still chose Lewis Carroll, E. Nesbit and Mrs Molesworth, or risked Ballantyne, Marryat, Henty and Stevenson. For serious reading there were Scott, Dickens, Bunyan and *The Swiss Family Robinson*.

The quickest way to see how far we have come since 1934 when the first Trease novel was published is to compare the *Times Literary Supplement* reviews of children's books in the thirties with specialist publications such as *Growing Point* and *The School Librarian*. Now we have children's libraries with librarians trained to read and discriminate by standards set earlier by Dorothy Neal White and Kathleen Lines. These same standards are upheld by the children's book publishers. Teachers whose training colleges are or should be stocked with children's books are exhorted to know and use the contemporary author. Schools make ever-increasing use of their libraries, and authors, aware of a seller's market, produce books to meet every demand as soon as it arises. Then they face the growing discrimination of reviewers and groups of parents who have banded together to circulate information about books, especially those for young children.

And the children? Here again we still find the assumption that all we need do is to put a good book into their hands and they are readers for life. It is, of course, not so. The revolution has been just as far-reaching in the young reader, and as Trease's stories are bound up with their fortunes and status, it is relevant to mention the most important changes: the development in the concept of reading ability and the increase in educational provision. Since the beginning of the century the belief in the need for functional literacy in the whole community has gradually become axiomatic. This now means more than the recognition of individual words; it takes for granted that reading is an extension of apperception, analogous to seeing and hearing, and that the reader will understand and judge the ideas received and act upon them, or enjoy for himself his own choice of creative writing. This was never otherwise in educated circles, but the extension of secondary education to others besides the middle classes was not something a children's author had deliberately to take into account before 1933. Geoffrey Trease's writing has matured alongside the development of reading habits in sections of the community which have little tradition of literary culture.

This process is by no means complete, and not all children reach the same level of reading ability. A child may have acquired by the age of ten sufficient basic skill to see him through his secondary school career. But what of those for whom reading offers no continuous source of satisfaction, or the others who are variously classified as slow, reluctant or backward readers? On this topic there now exists an immense body of knowledge and various experiments are currently in operation. Authors have been called to account if they concentrate on the literary and gifted child or pay no attention to the needs of a particular age-group. Emerging new authors are being encouraged to write specifically for the under-privileged and non-bookish child. The creative writer must, however, still remind the reading expert that it is by reading books that may be too 'advanced' for them, as well as the bulk of those aimed at their stage of development, that children become both competent and adventurous readers. The modern author must keep free from academic controversy on this subject and insist that his intention is artistic, that his first concern is to write good stories. But if he is totally unaware of the contemporary trends in reading studies, he may find this reflected in his sales.

The intelligent child, on the other hand, reads everything sooner than he once did. He becomes more easily bored with, or rushes quickly through, simple tales of action written for children and moves on to adult stories which have a strong plot action. Hence the continued popularity of Stevenson, Conan Doyle, Haggard and John Buchan, and the 'adoption' by the young of such novelists as Nevil Shute and Georgette Heyer. These children are a challenge to the author who finds them stimulating to write for, and many writers now produce books which make demands on young readers as searching as any adult novel. As a result we have a curious paradox: certain children's books are now discussed at High Tables and in Literary Societies. This is all to the good; every art needs its pacemakers.

Writers must also take account of the change in class structure which has followed the extension of educational provision. The picture of England that Paul Hazard said he could draw from the background of children's books in 1932 would not be the same today. A growing class mobility and a heightened class-consciousness are elements a writer cannot ignore if he is to contribute to the increasing series of books deliberately planned to confirm the readers' experience by depicting children 'just like us'. I once believed that the subtle imaginative process of identification enabled children to leap all barriers between their lives and those of the heroes. But recent research shows that non-bookish children expect on-the-spot transformations of their everyday surroundings (e.g. treasure in the back yard). They are more at home with the princely trappings of the fairy story than with those children who ride ponies and 'speak like books'. The problem now for the serious author is: are we bound to write for them what the researchers say they will read because it is 'like life'?

The amount of time now available for reading 'tales out of school' is less than it was, and only the bookish child who will read even with the television in front of him is the teacher's and the author's delight, for in him they see themselves when young. He is now the exception rather than the rule. For most children reading is agreeable, often exciting, if they find a book they like, and they do it willingly. But it is not the only way to get their vicarious experience, (and the interests of adolescents nowadays are active and social). Reading is only one of the many things the young now do. One knows that reading can still confirm and enlarge experience in a way entirely its own, especially in the world of the imagination. But the modern author no longer has a captive audience. He must take time from sport, clubs, TV serials, dramatics, amateur pop groups, dancing and idleness. He may succeed in cornering only a part of a dull lesson in class, but when he does, he must make the most of his opportunity and have something worth telling. Radio and television have played a part in bringing books to the notice of children and parents, but it is still the teacher who has most direct influence. The teacher will read out and maddeningly not finish an exciting incident which nags at an exasperated pupil until he has to get the book from the library. The book has to be worth the trouble; it must have something children want, need, or are stimulated by, or else it must not interrupt their games.

This is the situation into which Geoffrey Trease and his fellow writers have launched their books. On balance the writers can still win. The gloom with which those out of contact with the children's enthusiasm predict the downward trend of reading does not seem to be warranted.

Although the hack still lurks powerfully in the undergrowth of comics and pulp products, his standards and methods are exposed and ignorance is no longer an excuse for choosing a poor book. The outright purchase of the copyright of children's books has almost disappeared as a practice, and serious authors of books for children expect the same terms from publishers as are offered to other writers.

For at least thirty years Geoffrey Trease has played a leading part in this constantly evolving situation and he deserves more recognition than a short essay can give. He is, I believe, the most approachable professional writer for anyone concerned to make a study of writing for children by reading the stories rather than the histories of literature. I was such a person as he describes in *Tales out of School*.

' "Have a heart!" I hear some mistress say. "I have had a nerve-jangling day in the classroom, a strenuous afternoon on the hockey field, a row with a colleague and an exasperating five minutes with the Head. Now, having waded through that pile of exercise books, I am expected—this not being a night I have an evening class to take—to spend my last waking hours reading *A Pony for Penelope* or *Mystery at St Monica's . . .*!" '

But I could not cut myself off from my pupils' enthusiasm, and when in a later pile of exercise books I came across a reference to Mr Trease himself, I felt I was being accused. The essay was: 'The Person I should most like to meet'. The writer was nearly thirteen.

'The person I should most like to meet is Mr Geoffrey Trease. He writes exciting history stories and stories about children you can believe in. I wonder why we don't have them in school instead of history books and *David Copperfield . . .*'

72

Tales out of School was written in 1948 and extensively revised in 1964. Between these two dates the body of critical works about children's literature has increased beyond all expectation and this is, in some places, an academic field in its own right. But no other book conveys to the same extent an author's pleasure in his work and his concern for children's delight. It is still a vital and adequate statement of standards in writing for children. Recent investigations of how children understand what they read have made it clear that the dichotomy between what-children-like-to-read and what-teachers-think-they-ought-to-read persists where teachers know little of what is available for children and children expect school reading to be dull anyway. It is the modern author who can fill this gap if we are to make a literate generation of the children who compose the statistics of the great education reports.

Since the publication of his first book in 1934, Trease has made it quite clear that a children's author is an artist in his own right. This seemingly obvious definition of his role is not, even now, always accepted.

As a nineteenth-century moralist, an author could claim that the enjoyment of his books was in the satisfaction of evil punished and virtue rewarded. Sometimes a lady authoress strayed near the edge with the raptures and roses of vice, but the rue always followed. The moralists were succeeded by writers who set about telling a tale first, and their books for adults were seized on by boys in search of adventure and heroes. Then Marryat, Ballantyne and Henty realised that boys must have their own books and set about telling them stories, so that by the beginning of this century the writer for boys was a definite literary figure.

Why did he not remain so? First because the formula was easy to follow, and this discovery was accompanied by a false belief that whatever is designed for children is easier to do. Simpler vocabulary, thinner plots, less attention to accuracy and verisimilitude were the chief features of later adventure stories. Children who never get good books really do enjoy the bad ones, so the less scrupulous publisher and the hack writer and all the *commis-voyageurs* of book production increased the trade which flourished in newsagents' shops. These had their own clientele who never saw a real bookshop, and still do not.

Besides a false idea of simplification as the operative concept in providing for children, the notion that children lack *experience* was an unacknowledged preconception before about 1945. The fact is that they do not lack it, but their experience is organised to form a world-picture which differs considerably from that of adults, and which grown-ups speak of over-simply as a childish belief in fairies. Becoming grown-up means rearranging the material of this inner world to adjust ourselves to what we gradually discover to be the facts of the universe. The childhood pattern slips away as the adolescent begins to fulfil adult roles. The successful author presents children with an organised illusion which fits their stage of development, a world in which their experience is relevant. In England this has been done most successfully in a particular kind of fantasy writing, of which *Alice in Wonderland* is the prototype and *Tom's Midnight Garden* a recent example, and in the adventure story, historical or modern. In the first of these, time and place give way to a special mode of what Henry James calls 'felt life', and in the second the illusion depends on the characters being accepted as 'just like us'. At their best they are genuine literary kinds. Suzanne Langer says of them:

'These juvenile stories are most skilful poetic creations ... Their magic is fairly easy to analyse, and the analysis re-

veals what may, in fact, be found in any well-told story—
that the fabric of illusory events takes its appearance and
emotional value entirely from the way the statements
which actually compose the story are worded, the way the
sentences flow, stop, repeat, stand alone etc., the concentra-
tions and expansions of statement, the charged or denuded
words. The ways of telling make the place, the action, the
characters in fiction.'*

This is the challenge to the writer. He sees how the
illusion is created, and he knows that, for the most part,
unless he bores them with generalisation and abstraction, the
children will come with him. Does he then trouble to make
his writing consistent with any standard of integrity of what
is suitable for children and also integral in a work of art
judged by adult standards? The children cannot make this
judgment, and so many writers have assumed that it need
not be made. Geoffrey Trease stands out as the children's
author who has insisted that no other standard is appropriate.
He tells his fellow authors:

'An artist is what the children's writer *is*—a minor artist,
perhaps, but an artist none the less, though other people are
slow to admit it. For an artist's function is to interpret life,
and though the children's author has certain limitations, he
can still perform that function where it is most needed—for
who needs the help of an interpreter more than the boy and
girl? It is this status, as minor artists, that we should claim
and win in the *next* twenty-five years. (I don't think we have
it now)—but before claiming it we must earn it.'†

I am persuaded that Trease has more than earned the
status he claims. Since the appearance of *Tales out of School*
in 1949, and Kathleen Lines' *Four to Fourteen* in 1950, it

* S. Langer, *Feeling and Form*, Routledge & Kegan Paul, 1953, p. 298.
† G. Trease in an address to the Society of Authors, 4th Nov., 1958.

has been impossible for a children's author who has sought recognition for his work, other than a popular commercial one, to adopt lower standards. This also makes it the more interesting to see how Trease's work has measured up to his own rules and how far his books owe their success to their embodiment of his demands. Artistic integrity is an uneasy bedfellow with economic necessity, and it is possible to be idealistic if one is not dependent on a body of sales and a popularity rating. Current demand is a tyrant, and the output in the past of the children's author has always been large. Veracity in history is an expensive business not lightly undertaken; exactness in place description likewise. Like the teacher, the author is earning his bread and butter, and the temptation to earn it with a little less effort is strong for both and by both must be resisted. Children's books pay; there is no point in denying it. But if one ever slips into the fatal thought of 'only for children', one has crossed the line between the writer of integrity and the hack.

Trease has tried almost every kind except the strictly fanciful: adventure story, historical novel, travel book, straight history, review, criticism and radio play. He lectures to children and teachers and speaks generously of his competitors who have, in some cases, surpassed him in the work he inaugurated. In all this he continues to give pleasure to hundreds of children who know his latest books better than those who write articles about them. By his painstaking analysis of the task in hand he has given many teachers, librarians and parents help in asking themselves what they are really doing when they encourage children to read.

II. Early Work

Geoffrey Trease was born at Nottingham on the eleventh of
August 1909, the youngest son of a wine merchant, and went
to Nottingham High School. As a child he was the gluttonous
reader who delights and puzzles the experts, swallowing
fairy stories, the weeklies, the *Children's Newspaper*, bound
volumes of *Chums* and the Henty hordes without indigestion.
At eleven, he tells us, he was 'editing a form magazine running five serials from one term to the next'. Five years later
he was editing the school magazine as well as acting, debat-
ing and studying the Greek texts which helped him to win
his Classics scholarship to the Queen's College, Oxford.
This he resigned after a year. His determination to write
was apparently stronger than the attraction of Greats, and
in London in 1929 life did not have to break through a
cloistered academic seclusion; it was all around in a stark
form. Trease was first a social worker in an East End slum,
then a journalist, and he also taught in a private school.
The early thirties were the period of the writer-propagand-
ist, and Trease's early writings, like those of his distinguished contemporaries, show strong left-wing sympathies.

'At twenty I was selling guinea articles to small papers and
hawking an unpublishable novel round Bloomsbury and
Covent Garden. At twenty-four, all boats burnt, I was
trying every market from women's magazines to literary
reviews. I had, some time previously, come across Ilin's
documentary children's book, *Moscow has a Plan*. The idea
germinated slowly, and one day burst suddenly forth, that

77

children's books were not reflecting the changed values of
the age. Adult fiction was. Novelists in the nineteen-thirties
did not depict war as glorious or the British as a superior
race. Children's books had kept the pre-1914 outlook . . . I
wrote to a publisher whose list indicated probable sympathy,
and suggested several ideas, one being a realistic Robin
Hood story, in which the seamy side of Merrie England
should be displayed, and Robin represented as a kind of
premature Wat Tyler. . . The response to my suggestion
was of the kind which normally comes to young authors
only in their dreams—a letter by return post, saying that the
publisher had been looking for someone to do the job for
years, and promising to commission the story on a synopsis
and specimen chapters. So, almost accidentally, I became a
writer for children.'*

What began as almost an accident did not continue as a
second-best bet. In fact it was clear that to pay one's way
one avoided the children's market. The challenge lay in that
'children's books *were not reflecting the changed values of the
age*'; Orwell's version is: 'the clock had stopped at 1910'.

The reviewer of 'Books for the Young' in the *Times
Literary Supplement* for August 1930 praised Arthur
Ransome's *Swallows and Amazons* as 'unusually inventive
and lively'. The reviewer seemed to feel that this was something quite new in that he commended the 'sensible relatives
who had enough imagination and self-control to keep out of
the way of serious business on the island', but he had
nothing with which to compare it.

In 1931 Kastner's *Emil and the Detectives* went unre-
marked. Notices at this time gave preference to fairy stories,
and one detects in the reviewer's tone a feeling of relief that
he has to read, not write, these books. A good present for a
child was the standard pattern, and the *Monkey Moo Book*,

* *Tales out of School*, p. 26.

by a fellow of the Royal Society, was recommended as suitable for 'those recovering from spots'. Historical tales occasionally appeared and were praised if they were written in a manner 'which prevents the tale from savouring of the plain history lesson'. 'Children who can still be attracted by stories of the picturesque heroes of olden times will enjoy meeting Hereward the Wake. . .' The assumption behind this is interesting when one remembers what Geoffrey Trease has done for the historical novel for children. The reviewer's severest stricture occurs in a notice of a 'personal record' of the Great War written for boys. 'There are occasional weaknesses, such as the advice given to boys on their behaviour when in contact with those of birth and education lower than their own.' A story of a modern girl says that she 'found in "good old Britannia" a mother for the one she left behind and was very happy. The book seems to be a record of fact, and is illustrated with snapshots of scenes in London, Bournemouth, Devonshire and other British resorts.'

From our present sophistication it is easy to find this tone inappropriate, this handling inept. It is the more remarkable that Geoffrey Trease saw in this state of writing for children the chance he needed. His first published boys' story, *Bows against the Barons*, appeared in 1934, and is the realistic Robin Hood story referred to in the passage quoted above. Children were quick to grasp the point and the popularity of this early work continued after the war. In the preface to the second edition the author says: 'Boys and girls wrote from many parts of the world. The story was translated into Icelandic, and a friend told me how, when he was fighting in the Spanish Civil War, he found a German translation which had been published in Russia.'

The story is genuine black-and-white. The hero, Dickon, shot a deer after a day of provocation and ran off to Sherwood Forest, where, as in Shakespeare's Arden, we hear of winter and rough weather. The peasantry are oppressed by bailiffs, lords and abbots, squeezed for money, pressed for military service and they can do no more than put up a brave show of revolt. Robin Hood is celebrated not as the stereotyped romantic hero, but as someone who 'dreamed when the rest of us couldn't see further than our noses'. The heroic ideal shines through an impression of lurking danger. Children enjoy and respond to the clear-cut issues of right and wrong. At this time Trease believed that it was his duty to be a propagandist of social and political realism in opposition to those writers who trafficked in improbability. We find his villains capitalist in utterance, and the heroes are the downtrodden proletariat of the thirties rather than twelfth century peasants, but as an example of shaking up the mixture and telling a clear yarn it has still much to offer.

Trease is not without his debts in this and later books to the writers of the late nineteenth century who were sound plot artificers and purveyors of one genuine thrill per chapter. Stevenson showed how to shape an episode and to fashion a climax. He has insight into the fascination of a character like Long John Silver, the rogue who wins admiration 'as original as sin'. Teachers have never worried that the Treasure Island expedition was 'launched by greed and decorated with murder and treachery and concluded with luck rather than righteousness'.* Marryat had taught Stevenson that the real world captivated men and boys, while Ballantyne, Cooper and Kingston extended the frontiers of adventure, and morality had to take its chance with the tale. Above all, Henty carried the cult of 'manliness' through nearly seventy books of considerable length, and his recent revival is no accident. Dorothy Neal White says that

* Harvey Darton, *English Children's Books*, Second edition, C.U.P., 1958.

an analysis of the reasons for the survival of these writers would throw light on the popularity of Geoffrey Trease.

We have already hinted that boys want grown-up tales (but not modern adult novels), where the element of plot suspense is strong. It is a taste which persists in readers of detective fiction, although there intricacy of motive supplants action. Also, I wonder if the movement towards the perfect satisfaction of children's reading needs, the very appropriateness of the books now written for them, makes the danger of 'suitable' reading becoming yet another stereotype. The very incongruities of Henty and Jules Verne are attractive; they have the quirks and quiddities of real, not manufactured style, however peculiar. They make reading memorable, and for some children this is more enticing than the merely suitable.

This memorable quality the writers of the thirties failed to borrow from the major writers of boys' fiction. Harvey Darton says that at Henty's death half the juvenile publishers in London were advertising his successor, so clearly was the market stabilised. An idea of what these books did *not* provide, namely, a vivid picture of the active lives of boys and girls who became absorbed in special pursuits, brought fame and fortune to Arthur Ransome. Now the tide turned, and a new *genre* besides school stories and adventure appeared. Realism came to stay in a cloak of authenticity. With the exactness of a sailing expert and the economy of an artist, Ransome wrote of actual children in the place of swashbuckling prodigies. The illusion is created by loving attention to detail, a technique as old as *Robinson Crusoe*, and its very success made it a strong temptation for the imitator and publisher of stereotypes.

Trease grasped the appeal of realism and the effect of the adult story for boys. He next tried a school story. *The New*

House at Hardale appeared in the *Boy's Own Paper* in 1934, and in book form as late as 1953. The author says he was 'varying an old formula', but the variations extend beyond the limits of Gunby Hadath, although the familiar ingredients of house spirit, no smoking and rugger are all there. The theme concerns an attempt to make a new house out of all the individualists and misfits from other houses and touches some of the springs of what makes a community. Hard work, training and not taking offence are advocated. The characters have a kind of gentle earnestness which Trease's competence in handling the rougher side of school saves from seeming 'soft'. The masters are not blind nincompoops, but responsible adults who judge the facts of a case as they emerge. Those who let the house down are slack and selfish but not vicious. The dialogue 'dates', but this serves to point the difficulty of writing about young contemporaries. The 'bliss' of study tea remains in the school story long after Trease would have cut it out.

The school theme allowed for few variations, for the pattern was confined at that stage to the boarding school. (Other kinds were in the famous education reports which preceded the Act of 1944.) Mystery stories were fashionable, and Trease wrote several before his first adult novel, *Such Divinity*, was published in 1939.

Real progress seemed to be along the way of *Bows against the Barons*, in historical fiction which told a rattling good story and yet did more. The time dimension, the significance of past events, and above all, the involvement of the modern child in the past, would give depth to the adventure story and take it out of the region of sub-journalism. In *Comrades for the Charter* (1934) and *The Call to Arms* (1935) the propagandist element survives. These books are still of interest, for they are the first to treat historical themes from a viewpoint other than that of the establishment. Nowhere in history stories before Trease do we find any indication of what stirred up Englishmen, generation after generation, not always unsuccessfully, to assert that they were men with sovereign rights. What could appeal more to adolescents in their attempts to find themselves? Why, after all, should political consciousness be approved of in children's books only if it is the conservatism of Captain Johns? I am sorry that Orwell does not seem to have known *Comrades for the Charter*, the climax of which is the armed rising at Newport. Trease says of it:

'The general atmosphere of the 1930's gives a somewhat anachronistic flavour to this book. Too many phrases recall the *Daily Worker* of the 1930's rather than the Chartists of the 1830's. I knew very little English history in those days and shudder now to remember the blissful ignorance in which I wrote. Also, I believed in propaganda for even young readers. Now, and for many years, I have held that a children's writer should have the same sort of professional ethic as a teacher—whatever his personal beliefs, he mustn't use his position of professional advantage to press party politics on readers too immature to argue with him on fair terms. This is a difficult issue to live up to, sometimes because of the child's natural preference for black and white characters and clear-cut issues.'

Geoffrey Trease's later books give arguments for both sides, as we shall see, but right from the start the attraction of the historical story as he wrote it is in live issues, involvement, commitment, which alone, we are told, will save us from the sensationalism of the candy-floss world which Richard Hoggart describes in *The Uses of Literacy*.*

Commitment also means 'no writing down'. A system of

* R. Hoggart, *The Uses of Literacy*, Chatto, 1957.

adult values must operate. Recall again the tone of *The Times* reviewer quoted on p. 79. What self-respecting craftsman wants his work to be thus spoken of? The children's response was forthcoming, but a writer needs the criticism of his peers. How were they to be made to see that in the tale of everyday life the mainsprings of action are human emotions and personal relationships and involvements, that children feel and suffer, that realism is more than holiday expertise with boat and pony, that sticking to something that has to be done brings more satisfaction than good luck? Some of these points emerged in the first of the main history series, *In the Land of the Mogul* (1938), but they were unmistakable in *Cue for Treason*, and with it a new era in the adventure story opened.

We must consider it here, for it came at a significant moment in publishing history. Basil Blackwell was anxious to raise the standard of the adventure story, and L. A. G. Strong was the editor of a series the theme of which was 'thrills and decent writing'. C. Day Lewis also wrote for this series which helped to establish the necessary adult standards. The pattern of Trease's work was gradually being defined, and before the war interrupted his progress, he had pointed the way which he and others have since followed with success.

Set in the Elizabethan period, *Cue for Treason* begins with the dramatic throwing down of a wall with which a nobleman sought to enclose the common land. The 'statesmen' of Cumberland are ranged in opposition, but unfortunately young Peter Brownrigg is detected as having thrown a rock at Sir Philip's horse. He takes to the road to escape, and later, hiding in an inn, he is carried on to the stage in a coffin in a performance of *Richard III*. There follows his association with the strolling players and Kit Kirkstone, the girl boy-player. They later join Burbage's company, work for Shakespeare and become involved in unmasking a plot against the Queen.

This book has the marks of the later mature Trease history story as well as the crowded canvas of Henty. For the first time the traditional picture of Queen Bess is linked to the fate of her subjects at the limits of her realm in Cumberland. The songs, sonnets, dresses, play scenes are part of the real world which includes peel towers, lakes, hills and dangerous miners who are a law unto themselves. London is a fascinating but foul-smelling and dangerous place. The characters are round and full, especially the players and Boyd, the Secret Service agent. The gentle Shakespeare and the ruthless Cecil provide the shock of recognition, and the Queen is a sharp-witted old woman with a lot to worry her.

Right from the start the tale has movement, vitality and the suspense that comes from the loading of the circumstantial dice against the hero and heroine who must overcome genuine hazards with determination. The villain is more than a simple traitor, he is a usurper of rights. Trease the propagandist has now given way to the story-teller who has, nevertheless, been concerned to engage our sympathies for the oppressed.

Cue for Treason showed what could be done and how children would respond. They were delighted. The task was now to consolidate the position which had been so hardly won, and the adventure story took on a new lease of life.

III. The Historical Adventure Story

The historical adventure story, that strong-featured offspring of the English romantic revival, has sometimes suffered from its great initial success. The reaction against Gothic gloom, the longeurs of Scott, the anti-romantic view of history and debunking techniques in biography, increasing diffidence about empire building, and the thorough-going new look to which useful villains like King John are subjected, all helped to make historical novels in this century a dangerous quagmire for all but the intrepid or incurable. Only Queen Elizabeth and Joan of Arc have exercised a constant lure, and the French Revolution is a necessary subject for our writers at least once a generation, as if it were a touchstone by which we tested our own security.

We have already seen the state of children's historical fiction when Trease began to write, and that *Cue for Treason* is a landmark. Now the library shelves are crowded with historical tales written by authors of distinction; Rosemary Sutcliff, Cynthia Harnett, Rhoda Power, Ronald Welch, Henry Treece, Carola Oman and others, found in this kind the task most suited to their talents and interests. Plot there must be in the adventure story, but the old straightforward one offered too few variations, so now the writer exercises his skill in dealing with the extra dimension of historical sensibility. Gone are the days of Stanley Weyman when blocks of 'period writing' set the scene. Curiously, we are nearer Scott than ever, for he remains, at his best, the greatest exponent of the historical novel as an organic unity.

The exact nature of the illusion is what distinguishes the novelist from the historian. In supplying books for children between twelve and fifteen, history teachers have an identity of purpose with novelists which accounts for the delight with which good new novels are greeted by the discerning, who insist that imaginative response to the past is the foundation of a historical sense. But teachers make a mistake if they expect the novelist to do all the work. Young people do not mind, in fact they enjoy, learning from story books, but they distrust lessons disguised as stories. One can be very disappointed when a conscientious and scholarly work on fifteenth century coinage fails to 'take' because the plot is too thin to carry the weight of British Museum material. The pupils' reaction will be first and foremost to the story, of which the material of history is an element, the context of the experience. The writer is not to chart the stuff of the past in an enticing order, but to communicate its felt life. His characters live not because of the authenticity of their dress, but by reason of their truth to what we know life is like.

Yet we can now recommend novels in history lessons with safety because every reputable writer takes this for granted and also subscribes to Trease's stringent demands about accuracy. Not that one cannot write an attractive historical novel without research; the evidence is all to the contrary. But it is the more authentic a work if the details are right, and there is usually no reason for mistakes. Trease himself withdrew *Running Deer* from publication after discovering historical errors committed in good faith. Details of dress, food, building, sleeping habits, communications are not at the forefront of the child's mind as he reads, but they stick as the whole picture is built up; they are the organisation of the illusion and take the place of metaphor, as well as giving verisimilitude to the experience. Too many dress descriptions and they will be forgotten; too much teaching about the conditions of apprentices and the story is lost. Explain where necessary, and then as part of the flow, are the conclusions to be drawn from Trease's practice. Details such as how people washed, the whereabouts of the ancient roads in England and the repercussions of the Hanseatic League are indissolubly linked with complete experience in *Word to Caesar*, where water was a problem in Rome but not in Bath, *Mist over Athelney*, with its description of the Fosseway in winter, and *The Secret Fiord*, with its particularly exciting sea adventure.

Comparisons of how authors create their reconstructions of the past suggest that the differences lie in the kind of experience they want to communicate, and here the men are distinct from the women. Miss Harnett uses detail in a meticulous way which brings alive to the senses what medieval children saw, ate, rode in, played with, so that identification is a kind of domestication of the modern child in the Middle Ages. Miss Sutcliff penetrates a period feeling by strong evocation of colour, landscape and a poetic Zeitgeist, all in a firmly-welded prose which is in itself an experience, and therefore more accessible to the brighter child. Trease uses thematic material at once clearly local and nationally significant in a swift masculine sweep of plot. He suggests that men are prepared to defend first the place where they have their roots, and in the soil of England the historical patterns persist. The theme starts locally and branches out as national interests become clear.

This is particularly so in the novels which have links with *Cue for Treason*: *Silver Guard*, *The Grey Adventurer*, and *Trumpets in the West*. These three stories cover the period of the seventeenth century struggle between the King and Parliament, beginning with the Civil War and ending with the advent of William of Orange. Silver Guard is the house where the earlier hero and heroine had settled down and brought up their family, who in turn have to defend it from a Cavalier's attempts to seize it. Dick Caldwell, the grey, or Puritan adventurer, seeks his fortune in the new colonies when he finds himself homeless at the Restoration. The fated Monmouth rising is seen against the lives of a group of West Country children whose choice of careers takes them to the uncertainties and glories of the London of Wren and Purcell. No one runs away to have adventures because life is boring. Instead, the heroes are set on pursuing an even course; Gervase from Boston wants to avoid the Civil War and study medicine at Oxford; Jack wants to compose. When the political situation brings upheaval they say, 'let's have it, get it over, and have a chance to think about our own business for a change'. Now, if this is a device in novel writing like any other, it also shows a change of outlook on the nature of adventure. It suggests that men are, on the whole, home-loving and peaceful, but that there are certain conditions, oppression, wrong, intolerance, under which a quiet life is impossible. The adventures are a challenge to ideas as much as a love of fighting. Very characteristic of Trease's handling of detail is the inclusion of William Harvey reading his book at the battle of Edgehill.

This group of novels carries over the social awareness of *Bows against the Barons*. The emphasis is no longer propagandist, but an attempt to put the issues fairly before coming down on one side. The Roundhead cause is made an issue of principle, not a manifestation of Puritanical ill-will. The Cavaliers are no longer the heroes, yet neither are they all silk and show. King James II has few advocates, but he is given a fairer trial than he intended for the seven bishops. The real change in the shift of power to the middle classes is seen in the motives and arguments of Dr Pharaoh, the Bunyanesque character, for whose egalitarian ideas the pillory and galley bench are the inevitable reward. In *The Grey Adventurer* we see how attitudes grow out of a social pattern and persist after the pattern has broken down, as in the relation of master and man in the colonies and the famine that resulted from the failure to believe that the Indians could be trusted.

Without disregarding the need to present black and white issues to boys and girls, Geoffrey Trease succeeds in showing that judgment is not inherent in the events. Those who fought their king regarded it as a serious matter. Religious imposition and the conflict of conscience penetrated even the villages, and for some people, to go to America was a desperate remedy for a more desperate disease. Nor is this gloomy sociology. The vitality of youth permeates it all, and the sieges and battles have no less force and excitement for being described from the less usual (but winning!) side. Everything is not gloriously democratic in the end. 'There were a lot more rights and liberties to be fought for, undreamt of by William of Orange.'

Does it matter which side the novelist takes? Trease says it does. He adds that one must avoid 'the false general impression' which irresponsible books leave with their readers. He quotes the French Revolution as a case in point, where the English schoolboy has failed to grasp its significance for republican France because he is fed on tales of the Terror and he works out his concern in *The Thunder of Valmy*. He has also dealt with the Russian Revolution in *The White Nights of St Petersburg*. [We remember how Roosevelt's attitude to England still bore traces of his schooldays' teaching about George III.] Dorothy Neal White shows what has happened to the historical story in this respect:

'Reading a Trease story when one is an adult is mildly confusing because, vaguely remembering one's own childhood, one is surprised to find that the erstwhile "bad 'uns" have become the heroes.'

This also happens to historians and is entirely to be desired.

A different matter is the evocation of past events which sum up a whole period of vanished greatness, the large divisions of Greece, Rome and the Renaissance. What kind of an adventure did a boy have in fifth century Athens or under the Emperor Hadrian? What was England really like at the time of Alfred, that period which modern children see as a perpetual wet winter of low sunrises and great hardship with everyone living in the West of England? Trease writes here of Saxon Gloucester:

'They had taken the empty shell which Rome had left them, and filled it, not with a new city, but with a jumble of farms and cottages. Each lived inside his stockade, as though there were not friends and neighbours outside but prowling wolves of the forest. Where the ground permitted —where the spade did not yield Roman concrete, tile or brick—the Englishman made a garden or an orchard.'*

The challenge of these periods is to localise and penetrate the glories and grandeur by the same confirmation and extension of experience, confirmation in that the hero is young, subject to the restraints of his youth and his culture, extension in that the times had a particular vitality, and were not simply a succession of 'dark ages'.

Alexis, the hero of *The Crown of Violet*, is made to go to rhetoric lessons, but he prefers to listen to Socrates whose reputation is not high with Leon, Alexis' father. The plot of this book is a carefully-woven double-stranded one, involving a Spartan conspiracy against Athens and the winning

* *Mist over Athelney.*

entry in the drama festival. Alexis succeeds in both fields, and Corinna finds her long-lost parents. This stretched even a willing suspension of disbelief on first reading, but the motivation is sound and withstands any hesitancy on the part of the adult reader to accept so much success. Again, the strength lies in the historical context being carried along by the action. Alexis is a gifted young poet, but he is also a boy who has to persuade his father first that he is not troublesome and disobedient. If one thinks that the adults had no chance against the children, one is reconvinced by the soundness of the events: the children are caught when they meddle, and the adults have to be consulted and per-suaded before effective military action can be taken. It is an instructive exercise to knock on a plot in Trease's historical novels; they are made to withstand the carping of both children and adults.

The Crown of Violet was written after *The Hills of Varna* in which the last surviving manuscript of Alexis' play is discovered in 1509 in a Balkan monastery by Alan, a Cambridge scholar of sixteen. He is sent by Erasmus to Aldus Manutius in Venice and the tale unfolds with one adventure hard on another. Trease says of this one:

'The more I reached into the period, the more ideas came to my assistance. My youthful travellers would have to deal, I found, not only with unsympathetic and sinister monks, but with Adriatic pirates and Turkish janissaries, not to mention blood feuds in the Albanian hills. As their constant antagonist throughout the quest they had an Italian duke, one of those dog-in-the-manger bibliophiles of the Renais-sance who wanted the manuscript only to lock it up in his library and deny it to the printing press. There seemed ample historical authority for the most fantastic characters and incidents I could wish to invent.'*

* *Tales out of School*, p. 123.

The tale has a grip of excitement from start to finish. The feeling tone in this one is memorable in that it conveys just how great was the passion for the new learning. The duke is swayed by the argument that uncorrected copies of the book would bring the new studies into disrepute. The enthusiasm of the hero and heroine for Greek books is equivalent to the present-day devotion to space travel, and one hopes that the keenness for the sciences will find as good an outlet in a story which conveys the authentic nature of the interest as well as this one does the lasting devotion to the classics. The character of Aldus Manutius is also excellently done. Little first-hand information is available about this printer, so he intrigues the novelist and gives him the stimulus he requires.

The same kind of feeling tone, a sense of historical period made local, comes in *Word to Caesar*, where another journey is undertaken, this time from Bath to Rome. When his father's camp is attacked, Paul, the son of a Roman legionary in Britain, escapes with the help of Severus, a Roman poet in exile. Severus has been unjustly banished and can be reinstated only if the original copy of his poem is found to acquit him of a charge of slander against the Emperor. Paul goes by ship from Arles, which comes alive as a Roman port, and the evocation of place continues strongly in the Coliseum, in the Subura, at Baiæ and the Sabine farm which had once belonged to Horace. This story has the advantage of another clearly-drawn villain. The intensity of these period tales is due in part to the embodiment of the darker side of the peaks of western civilisation in those who flourish in deceit and treachery. Men like the millionaire Calvus, the Italian duke, and the foppish Hippias show economically and clearly the forces ranged against Roman law, the spread of enlightenment and Athenian democracy.

To counter the emotional poverty which, he says, is 'the saddest flaw in contemporary juvenile books', Trease makes the relationship of the hero and heroine a growing one. He faces the difficulties of writing about personal relationships with tact and sense, taking refuge neither in hilarious extrovert behaviour nor in sentimentality. Jack Norwood in *Trumpets in the West* knows that a baronet's daughter will not find it easy to marry a musician, who is regarded as 'not quite a gentleman'. After their exploit as *fratres coniurati* in looking for the manuscript, Alan and Angela must go their separate ways. Paul will not settle in Bath with Julia, but finds in Tonia a friend then a wife. Adults have come to see that unless these subjects are dealt with in books written for adolescents, their sons and daughters may look for them in a less attractive form elsewhere.

The difference in upbringing between boys and girls provides a good historical 'trace'. The girls are bright, intelligent and worthy of the adventures and able to hold their own, but they are not tomboys all the time; dresses and shoes are matters of concern when they should be. Whereas the boys initiate and carry through the action, the girls deal with people and the heightened sensibility is theirs. In *Mist over Athelney*, Elfwyn, taking money from the Danes, thinks he is taking part of what they had stolen from the English. Judith rejects it: 'one part of her mind told her that it was a low form of cleverness'. Girls used to read the books their brothers brought home: now they find themselves in the adventure story in their own right. Here is another instance of Trease's innovation: he introduced girl characters as active protagonists with their young male counterparts. Up till his day this hardly ever occurred: in John Masefield's *Martin Hyde* we have a significant exception, and here the girl (disguised) is Martin's opponent.

'One has only to think of girls like Marietta Strozzi,' Trease tells them, 'who broke away from her guardians at the age of eighteen, lived by herself in Florence, and had snowball matches by moonlight with the young gentlemen of that city; and Olympia Morata, who was lecturing on philosophy at Ferrara when she was sixteen.'

As the critics so anxiously remind us, the age of the hero is important. If they enjoy reading, children read books meant for twelve-year-olds at ten, and there is an uneasy probability about strenuous issues being settled by the under-elevens, however natural their inclination to escape from pre-occupation with intelligence tests to detective work. The historical novel takes this in its stride; children were adults sooner in the centuries before this. The author's difficulty is to temper the realistic wind. Disasters of the kind listed in the Prayer Book are too easily found in history. It is therefore refreshing to see that when two children set out to walk from Gloucester to Chippenham in the dead of winter their first calamity is to lose their way. The heroes have the hopes and fears of adolescents. A prisoner in Arles, Paul admits that he is afraid, and his first anxiety is to save himself, but as he owes his life to Severus, he thinks it sense that he should lose it by trying to help him. Trease has shown that by admitting fear, indecision and frailty as natural, and by calling on adults to help when their action only would be effective, one increases, not diminishes, the hero's stature.

With the decline of the infant prodigy has faded the nationalist distrust of 'the foreigner'. Here again Trease is implementing his own demands. 'In so far as the story writer allows himself to introduce typical foreigners, it is up to him to see that they are closer to truth than they have been in the past.' In *The Silken Secret* (1953), set in Derbyshire with more romantic trappings than most of the earlier books are allowed, the villain is an Italian employed as a landscape gardener. He is anxious to stop the silk merchant from introducing into England the silk-throwing techniques which are the monopoly of the Piedmontese. He has family and national pride, motives which cannot be dismissed as blackheartedness. This is one of the best features in an uneven book, which has the sureness of plot and memorable characters one has come to take for granted. There is also a greater number of stock devices here than in any other, highwaymen, gypsies who poison pies, stilettos, a maze and imprisonment in a cave, as if the author were trying to show that he could use them all and still bring off a creditable historical tale up to his own standard. I find myself watching the mechanism with respect, but do not feel this one vintage Trease. Perhaps this is the result of its having been written originally as a serial for the *Children's Newspaper*.

Nor is *The Barons' Hostage*, for all the success it had on Children's Hour and the support of history teachers. It is the most overtly didactic of the historical novels, a crowded feudal scene of 1263–65 in which all is bustle, war and government. The family involvements, through which the characters shine out as of old, are complicated, and the events of this confusing time are still confusing despite the excitement of the Lord Edward's escape and the stern character of Simon de Montfort. The shape of the story is held in more closely by the record of events, and although Trease has worked his brief to give boys and girls an idea of what it was like to live at this time (this tale is in a Phoenix Book series), he is more successful when he can thread his own chain of events and use the history as context rather than plot.

The style of adventure in *The Secret Fiord*, *Word to*

Caesar, and *Mist over Athelney* is characteristic of the later period. In *The Secret Fiord* Trease accepts his own challenge and introduces twins, running away, and the long-lost father, all the incidents which he has insisted are overdone in earlier children's books. Here, however, the motivation is strong enough to withstand these elements which avoid the obviousness of cliché. An unforgettable scene in a cathedral town involving the Corpus Christi play, and the escape from the Hanse merchants, show how entertainment and didacticism reinforce each other.

The apparent ease and clarity of outline of these later books owe much to the practised skill of the dialogue. This has always been the stumbling block of historical novelists whose attempts to recreate the contemporary speech of their characters is based on a mistaken imitation of the epic utterance of Meg Merrilees. A successful illusion is often disturbed by fake archaism. Trease says: 'If we accept the convention of Arabs, Eskimos and even Martians conversing in modern English, why should not Friar Tuck and Robin Hood do the same?' Another difficulty is the teachers' obsession with sentence structure. They beg children's novelists to help them in their campaign to make their pupils write in sentences. Here I urge my colleagues to give up a narrow interest for a wider one. Children must learn that there are many kinds of writing and many kinds of sentences, and if by reading Geoffrey Trease they write fast-moving dialogue, they will have learned a great deal. Also, a number of conventions have to be mastered before one is a competent adult reader, and it is just as much the function of an author to stretch his readers as to provide adequate examples of the taught grammatical rules. Dull, lifeless writing, however 'exact', is no substitute for a lively use of language.

'The two young people glanced back—the movement was instinctive, they could not help themselves. But the road behind them was an empty whiteness.

"There must be a village soon," said Elfwyn. "Keep a good look-out."

"I will."

"The very presence of those wolves is an encouraging sign——"

"Is it?" She was doubtful.

"Well, they're more likely to lurk round the neighbourhood where there are sheep and cattle——"

"Oh, of course. I see."

"Wolves have to live, like anyone else." '*

To combine dialogue and description and to make both organic in a fast-moving plot is to solve the major issues of the historical novel. To do this without loss of integrity and to win the favour of the young is to earn the respect of critics, the praise of parents and the gratitude of teachers. Geoffrey Trease not only fulfils his own demands in this field but also surpasses them in giving new life to an almost outmoded *genre* which was dying for lack of conviction about the adventure of ideas. The felt life of these books is undoubted. They have the vitality and gaiety as well as the idealism and seriousness of adolescence. In respecting his audience, Trease has won for children's stories an abiding recognition they were once about to lose.

. . . . .

An epilogue on 'real history'. The story-biographies included in *The Seven Queens of England*, *Seven Kings of England* and *Fortune my Foe*, follow the prescriptions in *Tales out of School* where the author speaks with feeling

* *Mist over Athelney.*

of both the attraction and difficulty of writing about Raleigh
and the childhood of kings and queens. Whereas the great
figures of the past enter the historical adventure story to
provide the 'shock of recognition', when they are the subject
of study, the writer, if he is a good historian, has what
George Kennan calls 'the virtue of being as close to what
actually occurred as human industry and conscience can
make it'. In writing history for young people, Trease steps
over the line which divides what is known from what is felt,
but with an integrity which illuminates rather than detracts
from the importance of the facts. The facts are for the text-
books, but they so rarely come alive without inspired
teaching. The greatness of Raleigh is enhanced by the way
he was subject to the frailties as well as the nobility of his age,
and much of what Queen Mary and Queen Elizabeth did
when they reigned is illuminated by their childhood
restraints and fears for which the text-books have no space.
These books fill the gap which separates history from life
and will keep an interest alive throughout the period of
wrestling with examinations.

The writing of historical fiction continues to set some of
the highest standards of writing for children and all of
Mr Trease's books which have appeared since this chapter
was first written have something distinctive. He now alter-
nates 'straight history' for adult readers, as in *The Italian
Story* and *The Grand Tour*, and for children, as in *This is
Your Century*, with fiction for both adults and children.
(In America *This is Your Century* was given the New York
Herald-Tribune Award for the best book of 1966 in the
twelve to sixteen age-group.) The result is a freshness of
approach in each new topic. For example, *The Runaway
Serf* is for children between seven and nine, an age-group
for which it is difficult to find convincing historical stories

as the 'simplification' of historical matters is a daunting process. But Geoffrey Trease knows that the story counts for most at this age, and this is a good example of what makes history attractive.

IV. *Tales out of School*

By the time *Tales out of School* appeared in January 1949, Geoffrey Trease had established himself as a writer in almost all of the kinds of books for children which he discusses. Before 1940 came a group of plays under the title *The Dragon who was Different*, and thereafter came the historical novels which confirmed his reputation: *Running Deer*, *The Grey Adventurer*, *Trumpets in the West*, *The Hills of Varna*, *Silver Guard*. A war-time spy story, *Black Night*, *Red Morning*, now seems to have a topicality and fire which remind one how much easier a real enemy makes the novelist's lot. A book for backward readers (*The Mystery of Moorside Farm*), a story biography of Raleigh, a travel book and the first of the Blackwell histories had all appeared before Trease formulated his views on the position of children's authors and the books they produced. A growing body of writing for children, parental ignorance and the prevalence of the 'sensation-without-commitment' comics, as well as an undefined, generalised concern about children's reading, served to make *Tales out of School* a tract for the times.

What makes a good children's book? Trease says it is one which 'uses language skilfully to entertain and represent reality, to stimulate the imagination or to educate the emotions'. Entertainment there must be, but that will never be all, for implicit values and standards will appear in the heroes, the language they use, the depth of response they call out. The adult will always include a measure of didacticism in his writing for children, if only from a conviction of his purpose. He should reinforce the work of the education-ist, although the teacher will look to him not to teach the lessons, but to help the process of adjustment, which is the business of growing up.

Tales out of School suggests, in sum, that the best books for children confirm and extend the child's own experience, whether the medium be fancy, historical novel, realistic novel, story biography or school story. They all need renewed contact with life to survive, as *The Otterbury Incident* of C. Day Lewis showed in the case of the school story. The same was true of the historical novel, and in this field Trease's work stands as a considerable achievement and has made this one of the most attractive kinds of writing for both readers and authors. As for the novel of 'children just like us', Trease later attempted to put his own views into operation, with intriguing results; great popularity with children and some reservations from adults.

The strength of *Tales out of School* lies in its definition of the areas of writing for children and the standards that apply to each, all, that is, except the curious hybrid to which we have referred, the children's story which is more popular with adults. The years which have followed the publication of this book have seen an implementing of some of Trease's ideas and modification of others. But no writer now uses twins, kills off parents, sets out on a treasure hunt or engages on any domestic, scientific or fantasy pursuit without remembering that his book will have to withstand the knocking of the critics whom Geoffrey Trease has trained. The publishers have learned quickly, the librarians have a valuable ally. Teachers of teachers, whose job it is to help young adults to understand adolescents by redis-covering the child within themselves, find the difficulties inherent in the task more quickly overcome when the students read books now written for children.

And the children, what of them? It would be a poor showing if all this concern left them with their comics. Is there any evidence that it has all been worth while? Enough, I think, to be encouraging. Every time a child reads a real book instead of a comic, something has been done. The bookish children have never been so fortunate, so that one finds that those who read a great deal become discriminating sooner, although they still swallow many things at once. For young people of thirteen and over, *Enjoying Books*, written in 1951, is excellent. To review a book for children one must give them a sample, not a snippet with questions for 'comprehension'. Here is a generous measure of all kinds. Trease's favourites come off best, such as Pepys and Raleigh, but if a child has any spark at all, it will kindle at the excerpt of the Secretary of the Admiralty digging up his buried gold. *Enjoying Books* will not be chosen by children for themselves: it should be in a library where it can be put into their hands when they are wondering where to go next. Here they will find that 'what I like to read' and 'what I ought to read' are one and the same.

v. 'Children just like us'

Formula fiction pays; this is the one certain fact that emerges from a study of writing done for children. Characters in stories for the very young, produced by a mind gifted with vivid eidetic imagery and a mill-wheel industriousness, proliferate in every kind of reading format and continue their existence on cornflake boxes, soap and sweaters. However much one despises the product of 'ruthless writing down',* one can be roused to fury, or emulation, by the size of some royalties. The situation is made more inflammable by writers of schoolbooks who have devised formulae for teaching children to read and write without more than a passing glance at real books or genuine incentives for writing. An author's claim that he has an educational purpose, and that rewards simply come, is sometimes a rationalisation which must stand between him and an honest examination of his motives.

The critic should have an altruism the author cannot always afford, but his temptations are just as real. School stories, mysteries and fiction families are easy butts, and the substance of many a witty paragraph has come from making old-boyism, pony pranks and bachelor uncles look ridiculous in the eyes of one's fellow adults. 'A boy amongst men and a man amongst boys', they can so easily sneer at the author who, until that moment, thought he was doing an honest job. They have spent so long in being uneasily superior, these reviewers, that they ignore the need to discern a real attempt to convey experience and to distinguish it from a

* Colin Welch, 'Dear Little Noddy', *Encounter*, January 1958.

recipe story. A feeling that one is stooping a little is sometimes compensated for by brusque detachment. It is not easy to apply adult standards to these stories and still feel that one is making adult judgments if one does not find them immature. In making his intentions clear, Trease helps both critic and author. We shall now see how 'the changed values of the age' are reflected in the modern stories, especially those in the Bannerdale series which appeared just after *Tales out of School.*

Trease had written formula fiction long before the war. We have already seen how *The New House at Hardale* improved the stereotype but left it unchanged in outline. After this came mystery and spy stories. *Mystery on the Moors*, *The Lakeland Mystery*, *Detectives of the Dales* depart from the usual mixture by introducing real scenery and the sense of actual location which came out so strongly later in the histories and again in the post-war moderns. These mysteries were neither better nor worse than the average for the thirties, although their bulky format now looks curiously old-fashioned and they are no longer in print. I am not sorry that the brittle adult humour has gone, and that the French girl with her curious English was not thought indispensable.

The out-and-out spy story, *Black Night, Red Morning* (1944) was allowed to lapse when it lost its topicality. The place this time is Russia, and the plot concerns the activity of Russian guerrillas against the Nazis. The urgency of war-time is on this story, and the hero is as heroic and the villain as blackhearted as one ever hopes to meet. It has dated too much to stand revival, but it has one of the most vivid of all Trease's arresting openings: 'I thought he was dead when they brought him to me . . .'

. . . . .

Another formula is thrust upon modern authors with a plea they are expected not to resist, that they should write for young people whose reading skills are less advanced than those of their contemporaries. These unfortunates are variously called slow, backward or reluctant readers, and there is a vague generalised belief that if only they could read, many of their social adjustment problems would be solved. The situation is not so simple nor so one-sided. Backward readers are sometimes quite content with their lot; their interests are active and social, not bookish, and once they are clear of the stigma of illiteracy, it takes a very good book to tempt them away from the comic or evening paper, and an even better one to make reading a habit with its own satisfaction.

Reading experts have bludgeoned publishers and authors to produce something better than stock situations from children's fiction with simplified sentence structure. Publishers are now convinced that the problem is big enough to warrant a series of special books, and these are beginning to appear. The author must have a clear picture of the young people who will read these books, the youth from the housing estate who has lost two years of school through chronic asthma, the girl whose father throws schoolbooks in the fire. They are the deprived readers (no one who really enjoys reading is ever reluctant about it) who need expert help, and, above all, more books which reflect their interests.

As a craftsman Trease has accepted this challenge. The stories in the book called *The Mystery of Moorside Farm* are stock tales, boy and girl protagonists in adventures concerning a farm, Nazi spies, and a theatrical family. The conventions stick out, the vocabulary is simplified, but the leap to the situations of the main characters is unreal for the backward readers I know, for, more than anything else, they lack experience of story telling. They need a different kind of illusion which gives the appearance of realism, and a quick succession of slapstick situations which produce a comic, custard-pie effect. This does not tempt the serious children's novelist. Trease's strength lies again in the dialogue. It is good that the book exists; we need so many and there are so few. A skilled author like Trease could improve on his earlier performance, but it is not easy to write effectively for the boys and girls, or rather, the young adults who appear regularly in the reports of probation officers.

. . . . .

Just after *Tales out of School* appeared *No Boats on Bannermere*. It must have been the most difficult book to write, coming hard on a definitive commitment as to what constituted the task in hand.

'When one begins to cater, like a school dietitian, adding up calories and checking off vitamins, then one begins to write down.' The catering in *No Boats on Bannermere* is too efficient to make it a good book, yet it is a great favourite with children. The others in the series, *Under Black Banner*, *Black Banner Players*, *Black Banner Abroad*, *The Gates of Bannerdale*, appeared at two-yearly intervals thereafter, and have come progressively into line with the accomplishment of the historical tales. While the early ones are just as popular with the children, it is on the last two that one should make definite judgments.

They are planned and intended to be stories of children 'just like us'. They are praised by many a librarian because, as one says, the children like a story in which the characters have a complete life, 'with school, home, Scouts or any other hobbies integrated but separate themes'. They reassure readers about a world in which other children go to school (day school), play with friends, devise schemes and above all suffer reverses and frustrations. As Trease himself says, the realisation that characters in books have the same feelings as ourselves is one of the turning points in life. In acknowledging this, the modern children's novelist has problems which E. Nesbit and Mrs Molesworth never dreamed of although doubtless they had others.

First, there is increased class consciousness, subtle yet sublimated by being discussed for weeks in the correspondence columns where the debate is overtly on the subject of the 'background' of children's books. Protests and retaliation about the middle-classness may not affect the child, but nannies and nurseries, tutors and country houses are hard to put across to children in the secondary modern. Trease is censured for making the Bannerdale children bring culture to the villages; they have a headmistresss who is an expert on Viking remains and a classical headmaster of the Arnold species. The answer is not to lower one's sights about scholarship, but to make the experiences ring true so that the surroundings do not seem to be the ultimate condition of the adventure. Scholarship is much less a middle-class concern than it was.

If the problem of class must be faced, so must the modern family, with all the weight of its socio-economic implications. The family has ceased to be a group of people bound together by ties of blood and has become the unit of a culture pattern, while the critics seize on the implications of the description of every chintz cover and every tin of beans. The school is all-important for the same reason. Since 1945 the confused drive for status in the name of education has brought the public system under the gaze of bemused or indignant parents and the partisan eye of the educationists. True, many a bad book has been written about a bad school, and teachers have had to struggle against the falsehoods that have spilled over from the school story into life, but I am a little weary of the children's novel as the scrapping pitch for inadequate educational theory. Trease, following the example set by Day Lewis's *Otterbury Incident*, sends his characters to day schools, but standards of good scholarship are the same no matter where, as Mr Kingsford, the Headmaster in the Bannerdale series, would be swift to point out. The boarding schools themselves have had to give up treasure hunts these days and concentrate as much on University entrance as the rest.

On the public conscience by reason of their colourful clothes, music, restlessness and spoilt-child-ness, adolescents are anxious to define their role. Their precocity is to be understood and acknowledged rather than bewailed, and in books as well as real life this involves conflict with parents, (hitherto, as Trease reminds us, conveniently dead), developing personal relationships beyond the stage of tomboy cameraderie, and frank treatment of sexual differences. All these things, Trease says, must appear in the modern novel for children in their teens. It is a realistic demand which, if not met, will drive readers to the supplies of the newsagent and the sub-culture of the railway bookstall. Do the features of modern adolescence combine to make a good story? Is a good young citizen an acceptable hero? This is a legitimate theme and a strong one, worthy of a novelist's best intentions. The story will, however, stand or fall by its overall imaginative conviction, not by the quality of its social awareness.

The volumes of the Bannerdale series vary in effectiveness. *No Boats* sets the scene: the Melbury family, Mum, Susan and Bill inherit a cottage in Bannerdale and go there to live.

Father is 'away' in Canada. He is referred to, but not hushedly, and he does not come back. His departure has left his family short of money. The friends are Tim Darren who wants to be a policeman, and Penny Morchard, whose father has a bookshop in Winthwaite, the nearest town. These are the main characters in each book together with the adults, Mr Kingsford, the Headmaster of the Grammar School, Miss Florey, the girls' Headmistress, Penny's father, the farmers, and Mr and Mrs Drake, retired actors from Sir Frank Benson's company.

To counter his own accusation that children in storybooks never grow up, Trease has taken the main four from 'eleven plus' to the career and undergraduate stage. Their adventures throughout each year are set against the normal round of term and holiday, and as GCE at 'O' and 'A' levels come in turn, so Bill and Tim, Sue and Penny rise from middle school to Sixth Form heights. Their responsibilities increase, the scope of their activities widens and their relationships deepen. The balance of home-loving Sue, motherless, harum-scarum Penny, practical Tim, and Bill the thoughtful organiser is a good one, and the reader's identification can shift from one to the other. The scenery of the lakes, the pleasant local feeling of the small town is what most children enjoy, although some in the heart of Manchester write to say that it is easy for anyone to have a good and adventurous time in the countryside.

Each book has a distinctive theme in this general background. *No Boats* sets out to make 'ordinary life meaningful and exciting', from going into a new house to discovering the ways of fell farmers. In *Under Black Banner* the friends are lost in the hills and discover a house which the War Office had requisitioned and then left to fall into disrepair. As it once belonged to the Nelsons whose son is the house sports captain, they resolve to try to win it back. Inspired by the Head's assertion that constant vigilance is the price of freedom, they set about wresting the property from the War Office, a task which moves from newspaper correspondence to tea on the terrace of the House of Commons. *Black Banner Players* introduces the two themes which persist in the later books in the series: amateur dramatics, and what the experts call 'adolescent social adjustment'. 'No girls at the Grammar' has always been Kingsford's dictum, and even although the school play is the worse for it, he sticks to his guns until Miss Florey wins him over on the score of a Christmas party in the house which serves as a field centre for both boys and girls. When the Headmaster protests, he is overwhelmed.

' "I can assure you, Mr Kingsford, it is just as irritating to me when one of my girls gets sentimental and silly and I find her work suffering. But you can't prevent that sort of thing by keeping young people apart. They *will* meet, whatever their parents say—or their schoolmasters! The question is, are they to meet sensibly and naturally, as they do here, or would you rather see them mooching round the town, giggling and whistling after each other?" '

A headmistress after every girl's heart. The trouble is that since the creation of Miss Florey, the real-life ones have been more severely judged, and some still refuse to take the hint. In this book the theme of how to become an author, the right way and the spurious way, is dealt with, and Bill has a chance to show his mettle when an eighteenth century diary comes to light and its publication augments the Drakes' small pension.

The general theme of *Black Banner Abroad* is foreign travel, which includes the particular intention of seeing why it is important and exciting for the young. Recollections of school parties abroad fill the reminiscences of journalist schoolmasters and school magazines, but this tale is written from the inside of the expedition. The four friends, now the mainstay of the Black Banner Players, a company formed from both schools, have two tasks, to play *Romeo and Juliet* in a Roman theatre in Provence and to find the French-woman from whom Willy the Waller stole fifty pounds just after the fall of France. The emphasis throughout is on growing personal relationships and widening experience. The book shows how, when young people go abroad, they become individuals in their own right for the first time, which is why their parents and teachers find them changed when they come back, especially if they have lived with another family. Like Bill, they may also have succumbed to the charms of Gigi, the bewitching character who, despite the author's control, nearly runs off with the story. Some of the best writing of the series is in this book; the performance of Shakespeare in the mothy dark of the amphitheatre is specially memorable. The growing awareness of deeper feelings is handled with forthrightness and tact.

Trease is always at his best when dealing with themes he cares about most. Although this is taken for granted in writing for adults, he would insist that it is also true of the children's author. The effect can be seen by comparing the earlier books with *The Gates of Bannerdale*. Scholarship, Oxford, historical research and the unforgettable perform-ance of *The Tempest*, are the mainstay of the volume which sees Bill, the grammar school boy with National Service behind him, installed after his scholarship ordeal in the college of his choice. Penny has fought the Latin bogy and won, and now they both grow up in a different social back-ground and move out into the world. Sue marries Johnny

Nelson and Tim joins the police force, so that Mum and Miss Florey can have a rest and Kingsford moves into honourable retirement. To the uninitiated, it all sounds most cosy; to those who have sought in vain the picture of school life for the majority of boys and girls since 1945, it is quite new. And it still cannot rest there; clamour will be raised until the unmentioned thousands who have not won grammar school places have their exploits recorded. The children's novelist will not be allowed to think that his work is done just because Geoffrey Trease has brought the school and family story up to date.

Bill is the teller of the tales, and as his chronological age increases, so, mercifully, does his prose style mature. This 'young author' is an uneasy convention to which a great deal must be sacrificed, and I am sure that not enough is gained to warrant it in the early stages, for the descriptive details show the adult author's hand. Sound as the theme is, *No Boats* has a somewhat stagey plot, and the reward motif, that touchstone for all adventure stories, is a disappointment, especially after the hard hitting in *Tales out of School*. One must not be entirely swayed by the book's popularity into thinking that it is better than it is. It stretches the reader least, and this is not the kind of popularity one covets for it.

When the real difficulties of adolescents begin, when their shortcomings have to be taken into account, then Trease rises to the occasion. Bill's disappointment when he realises that his poems are acceptable only to an unscrupulous publisher, his short temper about the schemes for finding the Frenchwoman, his jealousy of Penny's unknown admirer and later of his college friend, Penny's thoughtlessness, and all their moods give the plots and themes a precision of experience which the first two lack. Sir Alfred, as one reviewer puts it, is a 'cultural villain', and the obstacles to the successful manoeuvre with the War Office are not too convincing. Everyone is so kind and helpful, so *educative*, that I am happier when we pass on to the region of conflicting emotional and intellectual drives, away from the glad animal movements.

But to emphasise the weakness would be to detract from the real achievement of the series. It has implemented the idea that 'school attendance' has become a richer thing, 'school life'. To do this, Trease suggested that 'a handful of good stories might help', and this is exactly what he produced. Where before was a girl with a limp treated without sentimentality, or a rival tolerated because his standards of historical scholarship were sound? A boring and exasperating tutor is just as likely an inhabitant of a senior common room as a fine old scholar with great patience for the young, and the former presents the greater challenge in adjustment. The lucky accident rarely comes to the rescue of the plot, perhaps only when time and Gigi have stolen the show in *Black Banner Abroad* and the cottage has not been found. On this occasion it is worth it. Trease may not approve of the characters running away with the author, and the length of a children's novel rarely leaves room for it to happen, but this is a success. The class issue is never shirked, although it comes out most where it is most appropriate, at Oxford. The lack of money is what it always is, a nuisance.

The dialogue never really loses its sure touch, but it suffers most in *No Boats* where the curious 'simplification' is not worthy of the author's talent, and the reader is deceived by a false simplicity. I can understand a school-marmly complaint about this. It is much better later, but the problem of slang and the contemporary speech of the young is not yet solved; indeed it is perennial with all writers, and the adoption of a new medium, such as that used in *The*

Catcher in the Rye, seems to offer a different way of going about it. That is not how adolescents actually talk, but it recreates the illusion successfully, which is better than an unreal realism. Here is Bill discussing his part in *The Tempest*.

'When I tackled him privately afterwards he said: "Look here, old chap, the voice is the main thing out there. It's no good having the daintiest ballet dancer from Sadler's Wells if the words can't be heard in the open air. You're the best we've got, so you'll have to have a shot at it."

"Couldn't you get a girl?"

"Listen," said the producer sternly, "I'm casting Ariel, not Peter Pan. Some *Tempests* have had a female Ariel but this one won't. I'm allowed to borrow girls from outside to play Miranda and the goddesses in the Masque, but I'm not having one in this part."

"But—I'll have to sing."

"Yes, you'll have to sing."

"Am I *good* enough?" I said desperately. "Some people might think I was making the most unearthly row."

"Ariel is not an earthly person, so *that* will be all right. Seriously though, Melbury—don't worry. I wouldn't ask you to do the part if I didn't think you'd be adequate. Dash it all, man, I am producing the thing. You don't suppose I want it to be a flop any more than you do?" '*

The dialogue has to carry a firm load of description, the growth of character and more than a hint of didacticism. The pills are sometimes thinly coated, but easily swallowed. The town children must learn country ways, such as not throwing stones down potholes. With proper help the young write business letters, interview specialists, get in touch with the public services, all on legitimate occasions. They discuss careers, publishing, French food and how to order it,

* *The Gates of Bannerdale.*

university and how to get in. They learn how to do research and how to behave when invited to tea (go before you're unpopular). An English master gives a lesson on Pepys that would work, all in the to and fro of speech, which represents no mean achievement, despite some reservations.

A strong sense of values is the backbone of the series. Inherited formula is made meaningful by the clash of issues and different standards of integrity, or even keeping one's self-respect. Learning about different ways of life, about knowledge, and books, all add to the interest in making normal life exciting. Teachers need no longer shake their heads over the handling of adolescent relationships. The difference between boys and girls growing up, a feature we saw clearly in the histories, is skilfully dealt with. Here Bill shows the boy's obtuseness.

' "It's a sad case," said Mum, with something between a laugh and a sigh.

"How do you mean?"

"I suppose it's what you call in your grammar the *possessive* case . . ." As I still stared blankly she continued. "You rather like to feel that Penny is your particular friend . . . But you can't tie people down, Bill—least of all a person with her temperament. Possessiveness is no good, whether it's between friends of the same sex or the opposite. It's only a slightly less ugly name for jealousy."

"Oh, chuck it, Mum," I protested crossly. "I don't care twopence what friends Penny has. But she might have explained properly. It's the—the deceitfulness that gets under my skin."

"Naturally, darling, remembering the complete frank openness with which you explained your own day's doing!"

"That was different. There was a perfectly good reason why I didn't."

"Possibly *she* had one too."

. . . Mum was being, for once, unreasonable and there was no sense in arguing the point further.'*

No reader is deceived as to who is unreasonable.

As long as there are children's stories the adults will have to be put somewhere, so it is better if they can be accepted as part of the action. They have to be revolted against; it is not fair to the children otherwise. The Melbury children grow up by having to be responsible for their mother and to see that in the lonely dales they do not have all the fun, although like a good parent she allows herself to be banished to the sales in Manchester. She plays a real adult role, not too interfering, but offering advice when asked and being firm about the social conventions which make children acceptable guests. She shows clearly what Trease meant when he said that the mortality rate amongst parents and relatives was needlessly high. The most splendid uncle cannot be expected to go on being generous at a distance.

. . . . .

Does all this add up to 'making ordinary life exciting and meaningful' by confirming what adolescents know of it and stretching their imaginations? Certainly the characters are more 'like us' than books of twenty years earlier which avoided the actual situations around them. Despite claims to the contrary, I think that the good fortune of the school-boys and girls and their adventurous situations are no more than the average child might look for these days. Perhaps the young are not always so enterprising; one could wish they were, and the interest and support of the grown-ups is more than we might be able to take for granted in many real life situations. So much the better, if children are inspired and encouraged. There is a real danger nowadays

* *Black Banner Players.*

that their increased security may lessen their sense of adventure. Here, as in the histories, adventure is as much the result of an enquiring curiosity and a determination to see a job through as the good fortune to be lost on the moors at night, and those who complain that it could never happen to them have not read a set of ordinary children's compositions about what goes on in the neighbourhood at weekends.

The great gap filled by these books is the one between what children read in school and what they like to read, which we mentioned at the beginning. The later volumes stretch the reader without taking him away from the security of what he knows and recognises, and increase his awareness of the value of the experience which is already his, so that his response to life and to books will deepen. The Bannerdale books are not beyond the reach of fashion; they will date more quickly than the histories, but meanwhile they offer authentic imaginative experience. Teachers who are anxious to capitalise every bit of reading done by their pupils will find that they can boost a meagre diet and at the same time discuss with the same validity the issues which emerge in weightier works. Compared with more intricately psychological children's novels (*A Hundred Million Francs*), or avowedly 'poetic' tales (*A Grass Rope*), the Bannerdale books are imaginative documentary, carrying, as their author demands that they should, the readers 'from the love of romance to the appreciation of reality'.

Since Geoffrey Trease made his serious effort to write for the *contemporary* young there have been others who have achieved comparable and even surpassing success; but, as Trease began the movement of a new approach to the historical novel for children, so he should also be given the credit for experimenting with the new type of family story which is today a feature on many publishers' lists.

VI. Travel Fiction

'Fascinating and maddening by turns' is how Geoffrey Trease describes the 'mongrel art form' of the travel book written in a setting of fiction. His child heroes in 'The Young Traveller' series go to India, Pakistan and Greece with parents conveniently sent on jobs which give them a good excuse to pry around (films and university research), while to tour England in an old car they are joined by two other children from the Commonwealth who help them to see their own country with new eyes. One must remember that the intention is fact, not fiction, for the characters take an 'intelligent interest' sometimes bordering on precocity, and the quotation game can get a little out of hand in books as in real life. Adult readers are probably more sensitive to the mixture of the conventions and amazed by the amount of detail that the writer has managed to include without making it indigestible. Young readers take the setting easily for what it is, and move from sympathetic interest in the motherless son of a newspaper man to the details about the Acropolis without concern for the author, trusting that his craftsmanship will give them the interest and information they want. The facts emerge from the dialogue and from the description given by a character who has a claim to know about what he points out. For India and Greece, two places which he knows well, Trease has an unmistakable place sense which we have already seen in the novels. The historical and romantic elements which fire his imagination come out again in these books in a way which takes them out of the realms of ordinary guide books. The children note and enjoy the everyday things too, food, school, travel, as well as the special highlights of a Greek Easter and an Indian tiger hunt. All this is done with more than journalistic conscientiousness; it takes all his skill as an expert to produce a junior Baedeker.

In *The Young Traveller in England and Wales* Trease undertook a double task; to write for children who think they know their own country but more often do not, and for foreigners for whom the Underground and Welfare State are as strange as the Crown Jewels. Everyone will have his own complaint about omissions, but few books are fair to Swindon and the Chalk Downs as well as to the more post-card resorts. The National Trust and the Youth Hostels' Association are just right for this stage of travelling, and one is glad to see that children are encouraged to go off before they can afford three-star hotels.

Just as Geoffrey Trease's sense of place is capitalised in these travel books, his practised hand at dialogue is in demand when we think of plays for children. There are never enough for acting in school, and teachers who have thumbed their way through countless one-act unsuitables of 'The Bathroom Door' variety are delighted with *The Shadow of Spain* where their needs for many parts and sensible dialogue are efficiently met. The three plays in the book will keep the Junior Dramatic Club effectively busy and teach them a great deal about character portrayal and production. Perhaps the publishers should have issued the plays separately, as each caters for a specific classroom situation.

VII. Methods and Translations

Dependent though he may be on the tastes and interests of the young, the children's author cannot spend all his waking hours consulting their preferences. He examines their needs, takes account of the situation we outlined at the start, but he must also enlarge their scope, and, above all, write about what *he* likes if he is to give them anything worth while. Children trust Geoffrey Trease to do this, and it is clear from the letters he receives that while they are always anxious for 'another of the same' they will accept his judgment. They ask for more Bannerdale adventures or a story of what happened to Alexis on military service. 'It is very nice,' says one girl, 'to read about children you might meet in the street.' Although the letters are all responsible and grateful, they are not fulsome. The hand of the teacher who has begun to show them how to be discriminating is evident in a fair number. Some complain that it is not always possible to find all the books in the series in the library, and certainly when this study was in preparation it was impossible to rely on the local children's library for copies of the books. They were nearly always out, so they had to be tapped at the source before they reached the shelves. Publishers are hesitant to give figures and Geoffrey Trease is too modest to claim how widely he is read. The librarians testify regularly to his popularity.

Children are just as anxious as adults to know how a book is made, and they constantly ask for details and for help and encouragement in writing their own. Trease gives this picture of his background and work habits because, he says,

'I don't go in for midnight oil, temperament or self-conscious Inspiration'. Nor does he mention his infinite patience with teachers, lecturers, students and all those who take advantage of the fact that he is approachable, indulgent with his time and help, and concerned that the young should grow up into competent and sensitive readers. The secret of his work is meticulous craftsmanship and steady effort, a dramatist's eye for situation and a humanist's sympathy for his fellows. He shares with his predecessors in this series a capacity for humour and hard work.

'I now lead a quiet country life in Herefordshire. I have a pleasant little house at the foot of the Malvern Hills, with a typical English garden of very green grass and far too many weeds. My study is upstairs, with a fine panorama of the hills. My equipment is simple—a few rows of good reference books (on historical costume, social history, etc.) and a typewriter with which I write everything. I like to alternate periods of steady work with brief periods of lecturing or with journeys abroad—to collect authentic background material for some future story.'

In reply to questions about how a book comes to life he supplied these details:

'I decide on the theme—say a historical period I'm in love with or an event which makes a good story (Athelney, Prince Edward's escape from de Montfort) and which serves as a peg for something I want to say; in these cases that Anglo-Saxon England was a civilisation and a culture, not just a rude prelude to the Normans; and that mediaeval government worked like *this* and was subject to *these* considerations. I never go just for "a good story".

'I read round the theme, trying to distil a kind of essence for the story. While reading I make pretty copious notes on costume, food, vehicles, weapons, all kinds of social history.

I note, from real history, incidents and characters which can be used "straight" or in a fictionalised form. I choose settings I already know or can visit before the book. Special points have to be checked. For the horse-doping in Queen Anne's reign I went to my brother, a professor of pharmacognosy; for inquest procedure in *No Boats on Bannermere* I attended a coroner's court: just lately I have been getting advice from civil engineers and juvenile magistrates.

'I begin to shape the story. The climax has usually been in my head from the start. The characters are gradually moulded with their names, descriptions and mental attributes, not forgetting a clear conception of their pasts and futures outside the time limit of the story. I often modify the story in many ways as I go. Fresh ideas grow out of the original stem, and some of the earlier ideas have to be cut out because there is no longer space for them. Realising how much the story does develop while I am writing I don't always wait until the plan is complete. So long as I can see the finish of the story, I may sometimes dive in before I can see the whole route... My technique is pure "looking glass"... eat the cake first, then cut it, then bake it.

'I write the story on a typewriter. The opening pages are usually torn up and rewritten several times. After that, although I might go back and rewrite odd pages or even a whole chapter, I think that perhaps ninety per cent of my typescript used to go to the printer with no more than a few pen-and-ink cuts and alterations. Nowadays I seem to revise much more and I am very satisfied with 2,000 words on a good working day. For comparison G. A. Henty regarded 6,500 words as a good day, John Creasey (I believe) can do 11,000 in a morning. The actual writing of *The Hills of Varna* took five weeks. Nowadays with correspondence and other interruptions a similar book takes me about three months or longer. So the daily output is misleading.'

The first person to hear the story is his wife.

Translations of Geoffrey Trease's novels have appeared in French, German, Norwegian, Swedish, Icelandic Russian, Polish, Italian, Hebrew, Japanese, Estonian Rumanian, Portuguese, Dutch, Danish. This last is of *Mist over Athelney* in which the Danes are the enemy although the heroine's good sense in choosing as her husband, not her companion of the winter journey, but a young Dane, may have contributed much to this fair-minded gesture. There have also been German language editions in Austria, Switzerland, and long ago in Russia and separate American editions, Canadian school editions and German and Swedish school editions in English. A full length review of Trease's work appeared in Germany in 1957.*

Many of the translations are of the early, left-wing books Of the mature post-war books the most popular with foreign translators are *Word to Caesar*, *The Silken Secret*, *No Boats on Bannermere*, *The Young Traveller in England and Wales* and *The Young Traveller in India*.

. . . . .

The scope of this study does not include the recent adult novels—*Snared Nightingale* and *So Wild the Heart*. One cannot lay down rules for the movement of the young from juvenile to adult fiction, except to change the colour of the library ticket, but it is safe to hint that many Trease enthusiasts will have read these books before they leave school. They will find them really grown up, with new resources of wit, insight and imagination at which the children's books have already hinted, and they will not be disappointed if they look for the same enchantment.

* *Die Neuern Sprachen*, 12, Frankfurt, 1957.

VIII. Conclusion

Tales out of School ends with a chapter called 'To you—for action', and in the years which have passed Trease has increased the body of his work to an extent which puts him in the first category of writers for children. But more than that, he has made us all, writers, critics, teachers and parents alike, more and more aware of what is involved, and to what extent the children's writer takes on himself the task of helping to make the present generation literate. He has closed the gap between entertainment and didacticism, showing that in the children's story they merge happily together, and he has bridged the gulf between the comic and the classic in a way for which teachers can never be grateful enough. He has taught his fellow writers that if they are to earn their lauds as minor artists, only sound adult standards of integrity will do, all this with a seriousness of purpose and a sense of humour.

He will not rest on his laurels, and although the community will continue to make its demands and children to ask for another of the same he will take the lead rather than wait to be given one. The gap is now in our 'two cultures'. Our educational growing pains are not yet over as long as we have technologists who know nothing of the dreams and excitements of the period which initiated scientific enquiry, nor of Isaac Newton's preoccupation with heaven and hell. At the same time one cannot turn one's back on the atomic reactors. The children one now meets in the street are the sons and daughters of those who work there.

It is no mere extension of the habit of being, on the whole, laudatory and approving of writers of children's fiction that has produced this appreciation of his achievement. Geoffrey Trease has fully earned the status that he claims for himself and his fellow writers. The further development of his work is bound to add something to our awareness of what is involved in writing for children.

BIBLIOGRAPHY

Bibliography

Bows against the Barons, Martin Lawrence, 1934. Rev. Edn.
  Brockhampton Press, 1966
The New House at Hardale, serialised in *Boy's Own Paper*, 1934,
  Lutterworth Press, 1953
Comrades for the Charter, Martin Lawrence, 1934
The Call to Arms, Martin Lawrence, 1935
Walking in England, Fenland Press, 1935
Missing from Home, Lawrence & Wishart, 1937
Red Comet, Lawrence & Wishart, 1937
Mystery on the Moors, A. & C. Black, 1937
The Christmas Holiday Mystery, A. & C. Black, 1937, reprinted as
  The Lakeland Mystery
Detectives of the Dales, A. & C. Black, 1938
In the Land of the Mogul, Basil Blackwell, 1938
The Dragon who was Different, and other plays for children,
  Frederick Muller, 1938
Such Divinity, Chapman & Hall, 1939
After the Tempest, in *The Best One-Act Plays of 1938*, Harrap,
  1939
Only Natural, Chapman & Hall, 1940
Cue for Treason, Basil Blackwell, 1940
Running Deer, Harrap, 1941
The Grey Adventurer, Basil Blackwell, 1942
Black Night, Red Morning, Basil Blackwell, 1944
Trumpets in the West, Basil Blackwell, 1947
The Hills of Varna, Macmillan, 1948
Silver Guard, Basil Blackwell, 1948
The Mystery of Moorside Farm, Basil Blackwell, 1949, for back-
  ward readers
Fortune my Foe, Methuen, 1949
The Young Traveller in India and Pakistan, Phoenix House, 1949
Tales out of School, Heinemann, 17 January, 1949—the '1948'
  imprint is incorrect. Rev. edn. 1964

No Boats on Bannermere, Heinemann, 1949
The Secret Fiord, Macmillan, 1949
Under Black Banner, Heinemann, 1950
Enjoying Books, Phoenix House, 1951
Black Banner Players, Heinemann, 1952
The Crown of Violet, Macmillan, 1952
The Barons' Hostage, Phoenix House, 1952
The Seven Queens of England, Heinemann, 1953
The Young Traveller in England and Wales, Phoenix House,
    1953
The Silken Secret, Basil Blackwell, 1953
The Shadow of Spain, and other plays, Basil Blackwell, 1953
Black Banner Abroad, Heinemann, 1954
Seven Kings of England, Heinemann, 1955
The Young Traveller in Greece, Phoenix House, 1956
Word to Caesar, Macmillan, 1956
The Gates of Bannerdale, Heinemann, 1956
Snared Nightingale, Macmillan, 1957
Mist over Athelney, Macmillan, 1958
So Wild the Heart, Macmillan, 1959
Edward Elgar : Maker of Music, Macmillan, 1959
The Maythorn Story, Heinemann, 1960
Thunder of Valmy, Macmillan, 1960
The Young Writer, Nelson, 1961
Wolfgang Mozart, Macmillan, 1961
Change at Maythorn, Heinemann, 1962
The Italian Story, Macmillan, 1963
Follow My Black Plume, Macmillan, 1963
Seven Stages, Heinemann, 1964
A Thousand for Sicily, Macmillan, 1964
This Is Your Century, Heinemann, 1965
The Dutch Are Coming, Hamish Hamilton, 1965
Bent Is the Bow, Nelson, 1965
The Red Towers of Granada, Macmillan, 1966
The Grand Tour, Heinemann, 1967
The White Nights of St Petersburg, Macmillan, 1967
The Runaway Serf, Hamish Hamilton, 1968
Seven Sovereign Queens, Heinemann, 1968
Matthew Todd's Journal (editor), Heinemann, 1968

BIBLIOGRAPHY

G.T. has also translated two books by René Guillot,
Companions of Fortune, Oxford, 1952 and
The King's Corsair, Oxford, 1954
and has edited a collection of short stories,
Six of the Best, Basil Blackwell, 1955

J. M. Barrie

ROGER LANCELYN GREEN

To
Three Pirates
PETER COTES
LIONEL GADSDEN
WILLIAM LUFF
(Starkey, Captain Hook, Cecco)
whose friendship I owe
to
PETER PAN

CONTENTS

I Windows in Thrums, 137

II An Admirable Crichton, 148

III The Boy Who Wouldn't Grow Up, 160

IV Lob's Wood, 172

Bibliography, 183

1. Windows in Thrums

'To be born is to be wrecked on an island.' James Matthew Barrie was cast ashore on May 9, 1860, in a four-room cottage in the Brechin Road of the little town of Kirriemuir, seventeen miles north of Dundee, surrounded by some of the most beautiful country in Scotland. He was the third son and ninth child (but two daughters had died in infancy) of a handloom weaver, David Barrie, and his wife Margaret Ogilvy—so called, after the Scottish custom, by her family and friends even after her marriage. One more daughter, Maggie, was born three years later; but Alexander, the eldest of the family, was already at Aberdeen University in 1860, where he prospered so well that he soon became a master at Glasgow Academy, and before long one of the first of Her Majesty's Inspectors of Schools.

The Barrie household was typical of the God-fearing, industrious and ambitious Scots of the last two centuries, living in the strange combination of almost savage independence and a truly Christian sense of communal duty and fellowship so well depicted by Barrie in his later 'Thrums' novels. The driving ambition and enthusiasm for learning, which called out the utmost of application and self-denial in the family, would have sent all three of the Barrie sons to the University, though David and his wife and daughters had gone hungry to do so. Alec had already proved that such sacrifices were not made in vain, and David the second son showed every sign of succeeding as triumphantly in his bid for the Ministry, had he not slipped on the ice just before his fourteenth birthday, fractured his skull and died within the day.

Jamie Barrie was six at the time, and the tragic death of his mother's best loved son with all that it entailed was the most profound and far-reaching influence on his whole life and character of any that came to him in his childhood. Yet the influence could only have had its amazing effect on the child who was already endowed with the strange streak of genius that made him J. M. Barrie.

In *Margaret Ogilvy*, one of the most moving and revealing books ever written—and to many unreadably, even revoltingly so—Barrie tells of his mother's grief and prostration, of its shattering impact on himself, and of how he set about taking David's place and dedicating himself to bringing back her smile and to winning fame and fortune so that every joy and comfort could be heaped upon her. The initial determination and the plan for the golden future is common to many a small boy, even without the tragic incentive of a brother's death: the uncanny thing in Barrie's case is not so much the achievement in every detail—though this would seem wildly improbable were it fiction and not fact—as the unimaginable corollary that to do so he must remain in many essentials a child until it was done.

To read *Margaret Ogilvy* is to wonder also whether Barrie's mother did not remain to some extent a child also; but this is unsafe to assume, since we can now see her only through the magic glass of her son's description. And his curse throughout life, which was also the gift of genius which made him what he was, like that of his own *Sentimental Tommy*, was the over-vivid imagination which could so colour what he saw or felt or remembered, that the perfect picture became in the end indistinguishable to his mind from the truth: 'It's easy for you that has just one mind; but if you had as many minds as I have!' as he was to make Tommy cry in desperation.

Childhood was not all overshadowed by his self-imposed task of comforting Margaret Ogilvy, and Barrie enjoyed to the full the delights shared by his Kirriemuir contemporaries. In fact, when he was playing, he played more fully, we may assume, than any of them, entering into their games with the absorption and self-abandon which makes them so nearly real to the imaginative child.

To begin with there were the ordinary pranks that have been common from time immemorial. Barrie's friend of those days, James Robb (who later lent his name to a minor pirate in *Peter Pan*), remembered nearly seventy years later how they played at 'chickie mailie', as described in *Sentimental Tommy*:

'Into the woodwork of the east window they had thrust a pin, to which a button was tied, and the button was also attached to a long string. They hunkered afar off and pulled this string, and then the button tapped the death-rap on the window, and the sport was successful, for [the occupant] screamed.'

Or again, how they tricked one of the bailies of Kirriemuir who found a parcel lying in the middle of the Brechin Road, picked it up and proceeded with it under his arm—whence it was jerked suddenly and mysteriously by a long, unseen string, the other end of which was in Barrie's hand.

Among more lawful sports his favourite was already cricket, played at Kirriemuir with a home-made bat and a flat boulder set on end for a wicket. He developed the amazing straightness of eye and dexterity of hand which continued to astonish his friends throughout his life. He was, moreover, practically ambidextrous, being born left-handed but taught to use his right: long after, when suffering from acute scrivener's cramp, he began writing with his left hand which he soon learnt to do far more neatly than with his right. Being Barrie, he decided that he thought down his left arm in a more sinister vein than his right, and pointed to his later works, such as *Mary Rose* and *Farewell, Miss Julie Logan*, as a proof of this.

Neither chickie mailie nor cricket—nor the more mysterious games he mentions, such as peeries, preens, pilly and palaulays—were the most absorbing of the boy Jamie's occupations, however. His vivid imagination and the disconcerting power of mental shape-shifting found vent in make-believe of various kinds. Kirriemuir had a fine tradition of loyalty to 'the King over the water', and very soon Barrie was leading the last Jacobite rebellion, and was himself Prince Charlie hiding in a 'lair' above the little stream which flowed through the valley on the outskirts of the town, known as 'the Den'. The whole new page in Jacobite history is graphically described in *Sentimental Tommy*, and doubtless Barrie's imagination painted the scene so vividly that we might almost take as autobiographical Tommy's sentimental picture in *Tommy and Grizel* of Corp Shiach's vain search for 'the Den' to show to his own small son in after life:

'He set out blithely, but to his bewilderment he could not find the lair. It had not been a tiny hollow where muddy water gathered; he remembered an impregnable fortress full of men whose armour rattled as they came and went, so this could not be the lair. He had taken the wrong way to it, for the way was across a lagoon, up a deep-flowing river, then by horse till the rocky ledge terrified all four-footed things; no, up a grassy slope had never been the way . . .'

Other games took place in the little square washing-house (eight feet by six) behind his home in the Brechin

Road. These included dramatic adventures in which the final 'act' consisted of trying to put each other into the copper. In the Dedication to *Peter Pan* he wrote:

'This washing-house is not only the theatre of my first play, but has a still closer connection with Peter. It is the original of the little house the Lost Boys built in the Never, Never Land for Wendy, and the chief difference is that it never wore John's tall hat as a chimney. If Robb had owned a lum hat I have no doubt that it would have been placed on the washing-house.'

Most of these games of the imagination demanded some sort of background of a literary nature, and, as would be expected, Barrie was an early and an avid reader. Less expectedly, perhaps, others of the household read much and widely, beyond the usual careful and continual study of the Bible. His mother, Barrie tells us, was as keen a bookworm as he himself, and she 'with ten minutes to spare before the starch was ready would begin the *Decline and Fall*—and finish it, too, that winter'. They would read books together— '*Robinson Crusoe* being the first (and the second)'—and soon Barrie was deep in as many as he could lay hands on. He tells us:

'*The Pilgrim's Progress* we had in the house, and so enamoured of it was I that I turned our garden into Sloughs of Despond, with peasticks to represent Christian on his travels and a buffet-stool for his burden . . . Besides reading every book we could hire or borrow I also bought one now and again, and while buying (it was the occupation of weeks) I read, standing at the counter, most of the other books in the shop, which is perhaps the most exquisite way of reading. And I took in a magazine called *Sunshine*, the most delicious periodical, I am sure, of any day. It cost a halfpenny or a penny a month, and always, as I fondly remem-

ber, had a continued tale about the dearest girl, who sold
water-cress, which is a dainty not grown, and I suppose
never seen in my native town ... I know not whether it was
owing to her loitering on the way one month to an extent
flesh and blood could not bear, or because we had exhausted
the penny library, but one day I conceived a glorious idea:
why should I not write the tales myself? I did write them—
in the garret ... They were all tales of adventure (happiest
is he who writes of adventure), no characters were allowed
within it if I knew their like in the flesh, the scene lay in
unknown parts, desert islands, enchanted gardens, with
knights on black chargers, and round the first corner a lady
selling water-cress.'

By the time he began writing stories Barrie had begun his
formal education, though he learnt to read and write at
home. At the age of six he was attending the little mixed
school kept by the two Misses Adam whose father, a retired
clergyman, had come to live in Kirriemuir. This was the
basis of 'the Hanky School, which was for the genteel and
for the common who contemplated soaring' described in
Sentimental Tommy and, at one further remove, of the school
kept by the Misses Throssel in *Quality Street*.

After a year there, however, Barrie was removed to the
Free Church School to be drilled in the rudiments of
classical learning before proceeding to Glasgow Academy
where his brother Alec, who was now a master, had offered
to superintend his education and house him during term
time. He remained there for three years, returning when his
brother left the Academy, though not to Kirriemuir, since
his parents moved in 1871 to Forfar, five miles away. Steam
had come to Kirriemuir, and the old handloom weavers
were fast going out of work: 'Before I reached my tenth year
a giant entered my native place in the night and we woke to

find him in possession,' wrote Barrie. 'Where had formerly been but the click of the shuttle was soon the roar of "power", handlooms were pushed into a corner.' David Barrie, though he was fifty-five by now, uprooted himself at the right moment and obtained a job in the counting-house of a linen factory.

But he was away for less than two years, for in 1872 he returned to Kirriemuir, having done so well that he was made principal clerk at another new factory which was about to open there. This was a distinct step up, both as to position and income, and the Barries, instead of returning to 'The Tenements' in the Brechin Road, were able to buy 'Strath View' at the junction of the Glamis and Forfar roads: a strange, many-cornered house with a big window set in the angle with a view of both roads, and also down into Kirriemuir—the original 'Window in Thrums'.

After a few terms at Forfar, Barrie returned to the Kirriemuir school until he was thirteen, when his brother, now an Inspector of Schools for the Dumfries district in south-west Scotland, once again took charge of him for five years of uninterrupted education at Dumfries Academy, broken only by short holidays at 'Strath View'.

These years at Dumfries Barrie described afterwards as the happiest of his life. He worked hard, won prizes and enjoyed learning; he was good enough at organised games to pass muster with the more athletic boys; he could fight if necessary, but was more apt at making friends, with whom he went for long walks, visiting likely burns and lochs for trout-fishing, and ruined castles such as Torthowald and Thrieve for their romantic interest.

He read more and more widely (one of his school-friends was the son of the local bookseller, who gave him the run of the shop), revelling in the pirates and redskins of Ballantyne, Kingston and Ascott Hope, finding 'wrecked islands' in their pages and in those of Marryat and Jules Verne, secret codes in Edgar Allan Poe, more of the Wild West in Fenimore Cooper, before passing on by way of Dickens and Thackeray to the flaming style of the local 'great man', Thomas Carlyle (then living near Dumfries), whom he would waylay in an ecstasy of hero-worship, and then not dare to address.

In the earlier years at Dumfries the old games of the Kirriemuir 'Den' variety were revived and carried to thrilling extremes, usually in company with Hal and Stuart Gordon, sons of the Sheriff Clerk, in their pleasant and extensive garden at 'Moat Brae'. 'When the shades of night began to fall,' he and his friends, Barrie told a younger generation in a speech delivered at a Dumfries Academy prize-giving in 1924,

'. . . crept up walls and down trees and became pirates in a sort of Odyssey that was long afterwards to become the play of *Peter Pan*. For our escapades in a certain Dumfries garden, which is enchanted land to me, were certainly the genesis of that nefarious work.'

And as early as 1913 he had written in his Preface to a new edition of *The Coral Island*:

'It egged me on, not merely to be wrecked every Saturday for many months in a long-suffering garden, but to my first work of fiction, a record of our adventures, *The Log-Book*. We had a sufficiently mysterious cave, that had not been a cave until we named it, and here we grimly ate coconuts, stoned from the trees which not even Jack nor Ralph nor Peterkin would have recognised as likely to bear them.'

More important still was an awakening of interest in the drama and the writing of his first play. There was a theatre

in Dumfries, very small, but visited by London stars from
time to time—including J. L. Toole and George Shelton,
who were afterwards to act in several of his plays. The little
Dumfries theatre was, Barrie tells us:

'. . . the first I ever entered; so it was the one I liked best.
I entered many times in my schooldays . . . I had the good
fortune to frequent it in what was one of its great years
[1876–7]. . . It was in those schooldays that I had an
experience not always vouchsafed to greater mortals—I went
"behind the scenes" . . . Such doings led inevitably to the
forming of a dramatic club at school for which I wrote my
first play, *Bandelero the Bandit.*'

This was performed that same winter, accompanied by
two other plays 'based' on two favourites from Toole's
repertoire: for, as no copies were available, the company
re-wrote them from memory. Barrie played the heroine in
the 'vamped' version of John Poole's *Paul Pry*, on condition
he played the hero in C. Scott's *Off the Line. Bandelero*
came last—'a melodrama in six scenes and fifteen minutes,
in which I played all my favourite characters in fiction,
artfully rolled into one'.

But this was almost the last of the amateur theatricals.
In 1878 Barrie was eighteen, and having completed his
education at Dumfries but failed to obtain a scholarship,
he proceeded to Edinburgh University, still financed by his
devoted elder brother. The desire to write was now strong
upon him, still coupled with his devotion to the theatre,
and his brother seems to have had this in mind when Edinburgh was chosen, for there he came under David Masson,
one of the leading professors of Literature of the day: a
great teacher, a fine scholar and an accomplished man of
letters.

Barrie was already determined that Literature was to be

his profession, once he had taken his degree, in which it was only one of a variety of subjects. First, however, he must give almost his whole time to study for that degree to become a Master of Arts, and not let down those who had struggled to get him into a university at all. So for four years it was mainly, as he wrote in *Vagabond Students*:

> 'Grind, grind, grind,
> With eyelids heavy and red;
> A student sat in his lonely digs
> With a wet towel round his head.'

But writing was not altogether banished. Indeed, Barrie became a part-time professional journalist while still at the University, reviewing books and plays for *The Edinburgh Courant*, and even an occasional concert for *The Dumfries Herald*—though he was utterly un-musical. 'I can never tell one tune from another. I dislike music,' he confessed later to Rosaline Masson, the Professor's younger daughter, adding wryly, 'I was musical critic for several years!'

As the constant visits to theatres in his capacity of dramatic critic resulted in meeting several actors and managers, Barrie attempted another play, called *Bohemia* (with a scene set, of all unlikely places, in 'a glade in Brighton'). But none of his theatrical acquaintances showed any interest in it; the manuscript was flung aside, and he resumed his more serious studies.

He took his M.A. in April 1882, just before his twenty-second birthday, and after a summer in Kirriemuir returned to Edinburgh to combine desultory reviewing for the *Courant* with researches for a learned work on English Literature, which he felt that he must produce to prove that he was right in following his literary ambitions rather than reading Law.

But nothing came of it, and he returned to Kirriemuir at Christmas, anxious and dispirited, not knowing what to do—except that he was determined to be an author. Then his sister Jane Annie chanced to see an advertisement for a 'leader-writer' for *The Nottingham Journal*. Barrie applied in desperation (with a testimonial from Masson)—and was offered the post, at three pounds a week.

11. An Admirable Crichton

'What makes you write, Mr Barrie?' asked one of the child actresses during the first rehearsals of *Peter Pan*. 'Why, don't you know, Nibs?' he answered. 'My fingers are full of ink, and it *must* come out.'

The ink was needed as soon as Barrie arrived in Nottingham at the end of January 1883, with his first 'leader' scribbled on the end-papers of a copy of Horace during the journey. Five leaders a week were expected (average length twelve hundred words); but as if this was not enough, he was soon contributing book reviews, and then literary columns on Mondays and Thursdays. In addition to this a serial story called *Vagabond Students* in eleven parts appeared in the weekly supplement between June and August of that year; and his one-act farce, *Caught Napping: A Comedietta*, after occupying most of a page in the *Journal* on May 30, 1883, was reprinted in a little pamphlet—now the rarest of all Barrie's published works.

The play reflected Barrie's continuing interest in the theatre, and was written for the actress Minnie Palmer, who was playing in Nottingham and whom Barrie worshipped from afar. He seems actually to have met her and given her a copy of the play, but it was never acted and soon forgotten. Barrie continued to be susceptible to female charms, and worshipped quite a number of actresses in this way; but in their company he was overcome with shyness and could hardly utter a word. He was extremely self-conscious at this time, partly on account of his smallness (he was five foot one, and very slightly built), and was convinced of his insignificance to the female eye. 'The saddest words a broken-hearted young man can have applied to him' by a woman, he wrote in an anonymous article in 1887, 'is that he is "quite harmless".' Nevertheless, like the young journalist in *Caught Napping*, he could make 'a blush on a woman's face supply material for a half column paragraph', and many another subject too, as his prodigious industry grew and broadened.

There were no more plays and stories in *The Nottingham Journal* in 1884, but articles began to find their way into London periodicals towards the end of the year, so that he was not left quite destitute when his appointment finished suddenly at the end of October because the proprietors decided to substitute syndicated articles and dispense with their own leader-writer.

Barrie returned to Kirriemuir, and bombarded the London editors with long-distance articles. Frederick Greenwood of *The St James's Gazette*, in returning one, scribbled on it, 'But I liked that Scotch thing. Any more of those?' This had been 'An Auld Licht Community' which he published on November 17, 1884, and Barrie at once set to work on 'An Auld Licht Funeral', which appeared on January 9, 1885, and was followed by six others in the *St James's*, and as many in *Home Chimes* later that year.

Though Greenwood could give him no permanent commission, Barrie came to London at the end of March 1885, took a room near the British Museum, and flung himself into free-lance journalism with even more amazing industry than he had shown at Nottingham. The struggle was hard at first, and he may even have gone hungry on occasion; but within five years he was not only able to let journalism sink quietly into the background, but was hailed as one of the coming authors of the day.

Barrie's first book, the short topical skit *Better Dead*, appeared in November 1887 and he had still to pay for its publication. But W. Robertson Nicoll, editor of *The British Weekly*, for whom he was now writing the serial story afterwards published as *When a Man's Single*, suggested that he should collect and revise his sketches of the Auld Lichts, and was able to secure their publication in 1888 as *Auld Licht Idylls*.

With this book Barrie achieved immediate fame, increased by *When a Man's Single* at the end of the year. Positive celebrity followed when *A Window in Thrums*, a further collection of Auld Licht stories, appeared in the following July, and was confirmed when his Thrums novel, *The Little Minister*, was published in 1891.

Although Thrums is an almost accurate picture of Kirriemuir, the period of Barrie's stories and sketches is seldom that of his own youth. When as a small boy he first began his self-imposed task of comforting his mother and bringing back the smile which had fled at David's death, a ready way of achieving this was to lure her into telling stories of her own childhood. In *Margaret Ogilvy* he confesses:

'The reason my books deal with the past instead of with the life I myself have known is simply this, that I soon grow tired of writing tales unless I can see a little girl, of whom my mother has told me, wandering confidently through the pages. Such a grip has her memory of her girlhood had upon me since I was a boy of six . . .

'She was eight when her mother's death made her mistress of the house and mother to her little brother . . . She told me everything, and so my memories of our little red town are coloured by her memories. I knew it as it had been for generations, and suddenly I saw it change, and the transformation could not fail to strike a boy, for these first years are the most impressionable (nothing that happens after we are twelve matters very much); they are also the most vivid years when we look back . . . The new town is to me a glass through which I look at the old, the people I see passing up and down these wynds are less those I saw in my childhood than their fathers and mothers who did these things in the same way when my mother was young.'

The essential truth of Barrie's picture of Thrums is vouched for by Alexander Whyte (1836–1921), famous in his day as a preacher in Edinburgh, who was born at Kirriemuir of humbler parentage than Barrie himself:

'Mr Barrie has thoroughly grasped the characters of the little community, with all their humour and pathos. *Thrums* is a true picture of my native place.'

Margaret Ogilvy, who was also responsible for so much of the dialect, which was already dying out when Barrie was a boy, was herself brought up as a member of the Auld Licht Community (Barrie was a Free Churchman), her father being one of the leading followers of the 'Old Light' in Kirriemuir. The sect believed in a return to the early Church as described in the New Testament; their church was little more than a barn; music, hymns and written sermons were forbidden, and they chose their own ministers: the Auld Licht character 'was austere and fervent, but it lacked the graces'. An exact contemporary of Barrie's, whom I met nearly twenty years ago while I was touring Scotland in *Peter Pan*, remembered the Auld Lichts well and assured me that Barrie had by no means over-drawn them.

A Window in Thrums was more skilfully written than *Auld Licht Idylls*, but once again used separate sketches and did not make the rounded whole demanded of a novel— any more than did the picaresque romance of *When a*

Man's Single, which Barrie wrote one chapter ahead of the serial publication and based largely on his experiences as a journalist in Nottingham. But with *The Little Minister* he tried seriously to write a novel, set in Thrums in the early nineteenth century, and almost succeeded. Its great charm lies, as with all Barrie's works, in the style and characterisation; the slight and rather improbable plot cannot and should not try to stand alone. It turns on the young Auld Licht minister, Gavin Dishart, who falls in love with Babbie the gipsy, marries her 'over the tongs' in Romany style, and is besieged in his manse by the shocked elders of his congregation. All ends happily, however, when he shows his worth by rescuing one of them from a flooded river, and Babbie turns out to be the ward of the local laird, Lord Rintoul, from whom she has run away.

Meanwhile Barrie was toying once again with his second love, the theatre, and with more chance of success this time, though by no means at the first attempt. His dramatic career in London began with a play which his friend Marriott Watson planned to write about the eighteenth-century poet, Richard Savage. He asked his friend's help, and Barrie seems not to have done a great deal more than rewrite from Watson's script. *Richard Savage* was given a single matinée performance on April 16, 1891, without exciting any interest or finding a manager to give it a full production.

The next attempt, however, was much more successful, and opened on May 30 of the same year. It was a one-act play this time, by Barrie alone, a burlesque called *Ibsen's Ghost*, which J. L. Toole put on and acted in, supported by George Shelton and Irene Vanbrugh. This riotously funny sequel to *Hedda Gabler*, with topical references to other controversial plays which were on at the time, such as *A Doll's House* and Michel Carré's mime *L'Enfant Prodigue*,

made Toole eager for a full-length play by this new dramatist. Knowing so well what Toole's admirers would expect,
Barrie constructed a slight but most entertaining farce
called *Walker, London* ('Walker!' was a catchword at the
time for accusing someone of pulling one's leg) about a
barber who runs away on his wedding day to have the
honeymoon by himself and, masquerading as a famous
African explorer, is welcomed by a party of young people
spending a holiday in a houseboat on the Thames. After
many amusing situations he escapes, undetected until he is
actually leaving, when they shout after him for his address,
and he replies, 'Walker, London!' which they repeat,
realising they have been hoaxed, as the curtain falls.

Although the play ran for 511 performances, Barrie got
little from it but prestige value, as he had sold it outright
to Toole. But he set to work at once on another play, this
time for Sir Henry Irving, who had advised Toole to take
both *Ibsen's Ghost* and *Walker, London*, and wrote *The
Professor's Love Story*—a slight, preposterous and rather
sentimental comedy, but of great and enduring charm; the
first real example of the unique blend of humour, sentiment
and whimsicality, overlaying an unexpectedly deep and
universal problem, which constitutes the more tangible
aspects of Barrie's genius.

In this case the depths were but slight, and Irving considered the play too airy a bubble for the great traditions of
the Lyceum. Toole, Alexander and Hare followed suit, but
on Irving's recommendation the actor-manager E. S.
Willard bought the American rights and put it on in New
York on December 19, 1892, with great success. It did not
reach London for two years, but when Willard finally presented it there in June 1894, it ran for nearly six months,
and has twice been revived since then. It is not a play in

which the plot is important or can be epitomised, dealing simply with the charmingly absent-minded and unworldly Professor Goodwillie, who falls in love with his secretary without realising what the symptoms mean, runs away to Thrums from the titled lady who wants to marry him and is caught up in a merry and bucolic harvesting in which the proper couples are happily sorted out in time for the final curtain.

A great advance on this was the dramatic version of *The Little Minister*, in which plot and character are nicely balanced, with humour and charm to set off the pleasant 'period romance' of the whole. The action takes place in Thrums at the time of the Weavers' Riots (put back a few years to 1840) and the plot is far better constructed than that of the novel.

Once again, as with all Barrie's plays, a synopsis could do little justice to the literary and dramatic quality of the whole, which is a delight to read and absolute magic on the stage. This was Barrie's first really outstanding success both in England and America, and made over £80,000 in its first ten years. It ran for 320 performances (opening on November 6, 1897) at the Haymarket, with Cyril Maude as Gavin, and was revived several times, besides touring widely. It was immensely popular and well loved: 'a beautiful play, beautifully acted,' wrote Lewis Carroll in his diary a few weeks before his death, '*The Little Minister* is a play I should like to see again and again.'

Meanwhile, in 1894, Barrie had married Mary Ansell, the actress who played one of the girls in *Walker, London*, and settled in Gloucester Road, South Kensington—accompanied by the huge St Bernard dog, Porthos. Besides a one-act adaptation of some scenes from *Vanity Fair*, his only other dramatic venture, in 1893, had been the libretto of a comic opera in which Conan Doyle assisted with many of the lyrics. In the printed version Barrie added humorous marginalia supposed to be written by one of the characters, a small page-boy called Caddy. The opera was not a success, but Barrie was sufficiently philosophic about it to write for Doyle a clever little parody of a Sherlock Holmes story, called *The Adventure of the Two Collaborators*.

Doyle was a close friend at this time, and an early member of Barrie's team of amateur cricketers, the 'Allahakbarries', who played an occasional match against village elevens, and a regular one for many years running against a team of artists at Broadway in Gloucestershire. The name originated in the train on the way to the first match, when Barrie found it necessary to instruct more than one of his players 'in the finesse of the game: which was the side of the bat you hit with, for instance'. Two of the team were African explorers, and Barrie asked Joseph Thomson what was the Arabic for 'Heaven help us'. The answer being 'Allah akbar', a title for the team was found without difficulty. Doyle was the only really good player in the Allahakbarries, though A. E. W. Mason proved himself a good fast bowler; but of the rest Barrie wrote that 'the more distinguished as authors his men were the worse they played,' and described how 'Maurice Hewlett could sometimes look well set just before he came out,' or 'Charles Whibley threw in unerringly but in the wrong direction.'

Before the success of his plays turned him wholly to the theatre, Barrie continued to write novels; and indeed some critics regretted that he ever succumbed to the glamour of the stage which, as Doyle for example held, 'diverted from literature the man with the purest style of his age'. The novels did not come very easily, however, and after *The Little Minister* it was nearly five years before the next was ready, and even then it had run away with Barrie to such an extent that he had to issue the story of his hero's boyhood as *Sentimental Tommy* in 1896 and keep the rest of his scheme for a sequel.

It was a long, strange book with very little shape, telling how Tommy Sandys began his life in a London slum, and, on his mother's death, was brought to Thrums with his baby sister Elspeth. Tommy's boyhood is studied in detail, with entrancing descriptions of the imaginative games which he organised with Elspeth, his faithful friend Corp and the lonely little girl Grizel, daughter of another outcast, the 'Painted Lady'. But the underlying study is of Tommy's character—which might under less happy circumstances have been that of Barrie himself, who could see so clearly the dangers besetting the dreamer, the escapist and the creative artist blessed—or cursed—with the imaginative temperament which was his own penalty of genius. 'He had a devouring desire to try on other folks' feelings, as if they were so many suits of clothes,' says the schoolmaster of Tommy.

Despite the boyish delight in all Tommy's youthful ploys and imaginings, there was a slight undertone of bitterness which surprised readers who expected the frank romanticism of *The Little Minister*. But when the sequel, *Tommy and Grizel*, appeared in 1900 the escapists received a very rude shock indeed: for the book is stark tragedy and almost brutally merciless as it probes into Tommy's failure to grow up and come to grips with adult life, to face reality squarely instead of shying off into the imagined situations in which such as Tommy hide from the world.

'Poor Tommy! he was still a boy, he was ever a boy, trying sometimes, as now, to be a man, and always when he looked round he ran back to his boyhood as if he saw it holding out its arms to him and inviting him to come back and play. He was so fond of being a boy that he could not grow up.'

In spite of its obvious relation to *Peter Pan*, *Tommy and Grizel* must not be taken as autobiographical, except to the extent that Barrie was the kind of man who could experience enough of Tommy's particular tragedy to understand it and follow it to the conclusions which he himself never approached. Like Tommy, he might have said of it:

'I had no say in the matter; the thing demanded of me that I should do it and I had to do it.'

The urge which produced *Tommy and Grizel* led Barrie in 1900 to write his only problem play, *The Wedding Guest*, though plays of the kind were popular at the time, the influence of Ibsen having affected even such dramatists as Wilde and Pinero, while laying the foundations for the theatre of Shaw and Galsworthy.

'Ibsen? Queer now to think that Ibsen was once considered advanced!' says the New Man in Barrie's one-act skit, *Punch*, produced in 1906. Barrie's problem play of the mistress (plus baby) who turns up at her ex-lover's wedding, and then denounces him to the over-sheltered bride, is good strong stuff of the kind then demanded, but was either too 'advanced' or not convincingly worked out: it ran for only a hundred performances and has not been revived.

Then, wisely, he turned back to the romance and charm which had captivated so many audiences in *The Little Minister* and wrote *Quality Street*—as fragile as egg-shell china and as delicate. Set in the Napoleonic period with a background that recalls *Cranford*, it is an artificial comedy of great theatrical skill, and yet real and poignant even in this very different age. For Phoebe's problem when 'the gallant Captain Brown' returns after ten years to find her so changed and aged, is a real and universal one, in spite of the setting; and her instinctive solution of it is perfectly true to life—even if in life such situations do not often reach so happy an outcome.

Quality Street is still one of Barrie's most popular plays, both on the professional and amateur stages. In the published version, with his amusing stage directions, it reads as a pleasant, rather romantic 'period' story, and is a particular favourite with younger readers—girls, perhaps, rather than boys.

The next play, one of Barrie's most completely successful and one of the two or three which give him an assured place among our greater dramatists, was *The Admirable Crichton*, also produced in 1902, about six weeks after *Quality Street*. The basic idea came from a suggestion made by Conan Doyle while staying with Barrie at Kirriemuir in 1893: 'If a king and an able seaman were wrecked together on a desert island for the rest of their lives, the sailor would end as king and the monarch as his servant.' From this grew Barrie's parable of the Earl of Loam and his party, cast away on their island and helpless in this new setting until Crichton the butler, who in the first act has been the perfect servant in an aristocratic household, takes control and shows himself to be the natural master in the given circumstances. By the end of the third act the situation is approaching its remorsely logical conclusion, with Crichton as undisputed king about to choose the Earl's eldest daughter as his bride, when the rescue party reaches the island—summoned by Crichton who fires the beacon at the supreme moment, though he knows what the result will be. In the last act Crichton is once more the butler in Lord Loam's Mayfair house, while all the party have slipped back into their original characters, and their reactions to the island adventure point the moral and underline the quiet satire on the values of civilisation.

'It deals,' remarked the old actor Sir Squire Bancroft in melancholy tones to A. E. W. Mason after the first night, 'with the juxtaposition of the drawing-room and the servants' hall—always to me a very painful subject.'

III. The Boy Who Wouldn't Grow Up

All Barrie's life led up to the creation of Peter Pan, and everything that he had written so far contained hints or foreshadowings of what was to come. Sentimental Tommy himself had devised the first draft for the story:

'It was but a reverie about a little boy who was lost. His parents find him in a wood singing joyfully to himself because he thinks he can now be a boy for ever; and he fears that if they catch him they will compel him to grow into a man, so he runs farther from them into the wood and is running still, singing to himself because he is always to be a boy.'

Peter Pan holds a peculiar position: his is the only story of recent centuries to escape from literature into folklore. For every one person who has seen the play or read the story there are hundreds who know perfectly well who and what Peter Pan is. Besides being a fairy-tale character, he is also a symbol—of what, precisely, even Barrie could not find words to describe: 'I'm youth, I'm joy! I'm a little bird that has broken out of the egg!' cries Peter—and Hook cannot understand, but says blankly, 'Oh . . . Well, to it again,' as he raises his cutlass.

Peter Pan was created in Kensington Gardens, in the course of stories told to a party of small boys day after day and week after week: but how he began neither Barrie nor any of them could ever remember. 'I made Peter by rubbing the five of you violently together, as savages with two sticks produce a flame.'

The boys were the children of Arthur Llewelyn Davies

and Sylvia, the daughter of George du Maurier and sister of Gerald, who played Captain Hook and many other leads in Barrie's plays. Barrie, with his big dog Porthos, met them in the Gardens and told stories that began with the old fairy tales and wandered away, in and out of legend and literature, introducing himself, Porthos, the boys and occasionally other young friends. From four years of story-telling grew his oddest book, the jumble of whimsy, magic and delight called *The Little White Bird* (1902), six chapters of which were afterwards extracted and accompanied by the finest of all Arthur Rackham's illustrations under the title of *Peter Pan in Kensington Gardens* (1906).

For anyone brought up on this book Kensington Gardens has become an extra province of Fairyland. It is hard to believe that the bird sanctuary in the Serpentine was ever known as anything but Peter Pan's Island, and in 1954 *The Times* recognised his ownership in an article on the restoration of the chains intended to keep all human visitors from its shores:

'This is the island on which Peter Pan used to land in his nightly adventures, and perhaps he still does so; but the Ministry of Works have not extended the privilege to anyone else.'

These adventures of Peter Pan precede those in the Never, Never Land: 'I ran away the day I was born,' he tells Wendy. 'I want always to be a little boy and to have fun. So I ran away to Kensington Gardens and lived a long, long time among the fairies.' *The Little White Bird* was for adults, and writing rather quizzically of the little boy David for whom the stories are supposed to be told, Barrie develops the small child's myth that babies were birds before being sent to their mothers. For this reason Peter Pan is a baby whom his mother forgets to weigh, so that he can still fly. When running, or rather flying, away he naturally returns to the island in the Serpentine from which he came, and is marooned there as soon as he realises he is not a bird: with loss of faith he loses the power of flight. The birds build the Thrush's Nest for him to sail to the Gardens, and he becomes the Fairies' playfellow, his main adventure being when he meets the little girl Maimie, who hides after the gates are shut with the object of seeing him. It is for her that the first Wendy House is built by the fairies, when she falls asleep in the snow; and it is because he is still only a baby that Peter Pan, who knows no better, holds out his hand for a kiss and puts up his face for a thimble.

At the end of *The Little White Bird* the narrator retains David's allegiance by moving on from fairy tales to stories of 'wrecked islands'; and this exactly parallels the growth of the legend—and of the Davies boys. For in 1901 they came to stay near Tilford in Surrey, only a little way from the house on the shore of the Black Lake which the Barries had bought the previous summer.

The stories were resumed, but were now concerned with pirates, redskins and desert islands; there were games besides stories, and Barrie took numerous photographs of the three elder boys—'We set out to be wrecked'—with Porthos in attendance, sometimes masquerading as a tiger. An old suit and a black mask roughly stuffed with bracken served for 'the pirate Swarthy', to be strung up in the final moment of triumph.

After the holiday Barrie prepared a book to celebrate it, of which only two copies were printed, called *The Boy Castaways of Black Lake Island*, bound to resemble the early editions of *Treasure Island* and consisting of a Preface and List of Chapters parodying such stories as *The Swiss*

Family Robinson and *The Coral Island*; but instead of text there are only the thirty-six photographs, each with a suitable caption.

A chance visit to the theatre with the Davies boys to see Seymour Hicks and Ellaline Terriss (who had played Valentine Brown and Phoebe Throssel) in their own children's entertainment, *Bluebell in Fairyland*, at Christmas 1901 turned Barrie's thoughts towards writing a play for children himself. With *The Little White Bird* off his hands at the end of the summer of 1902, he began revolving ideas and making notes: 'What children like best is imitation of real boys and girls (not so much *comic* business),' which pointed out the weakness in *Bluebell*. Then came an actual line spoken by Peter Davies, 'Mother, how did we get to know you?' and the sudden recollection of Tommy Sandys's story: 'Play: "The Happy Boy": boy who couldn't grow up—runs away from pain and death—is caught *wild*...'

The Boy was obviously Peter Pan; the children would be modelled on those boys whom he knew most intimately, George and John and Peter and Michael and Nicholas... Then *The Boy Castaways* fell into place, Peter Pan grew to their age but was never to grow any older, and the outlines of the play began to unfold themselves before him.

There must be a heroine, a younger and more innocent Grizel whom Peter Pan could only think of as his mother— and an early child friend, W. E. Henley's little daughter, Margaret, stepped into place. She had made a very special impression on Barrie before her tragic death at the age of five— 'one might call it a sudden idea that came to her in the middle of her romping'—and he had already enshrined her as the child Reddy in the early chapters of *Sentimental Tommy*. But now she was to find her place in folklore, with a name that had never been heard before: 'You my fwendy—I your little "wendy",' she had said to Barrie, and a new name was born.

Now the story was growing; Barrie insisted that what he used was only a fraction of what was there, but he alone could draw out the very essence of childhood and the imaginative world into which most children can retire. Perhaps it was because he himself could still slip away—escape, if you like—for brief moments into that world. Unlike Tommy, he could still find the golden ladder into it, even if, in the world of everyday, some penalty must be demanded of him as the price of readmission.

Fairy tale and adventure story, legend and history, yielded scraps of coloured glass that would fall into place in the kaleidoscope of his mind to form the picture that was to be *Peter Pan*. Real chronicles of the buccaneers, besides *Treasure Island* and the 'penny dreadfuls' of his schooldays, yielded up the pirates; *Peter Schlemihl* the detachable shadow; 'wrecked islands' innumerable loomed above the horizon from Crusoe to Crichton; Good Dog Tray sat down to Frederick's dinner in *Struwwelpeter*—but Porthos had actually assumed the shape of William Paterson in *The Little White Bird*. Maimie's fairy dwelling was ready to be built as soon as Wendy should sing:

'I wish I had a darling house,
    The littlest ever seen,
With funny little red walls
    And roof of mossy green.'

while the children who fell out of their perambulators were ready to grow into Lost Boys and become Peter's followers in the Never, Never Land—a name which detached itself automatically from a real district in Australia to become the one and only island of eternal make-believe.

But the essentials were all the old dreams of children and

story-tellers since the world began: to fly, to run away from
the responsibilities of growing up and yet to assume all the
prerogatives of the grown-up, to fight without being hurt,
to kill without shedding blood or causing pain, to flirt with
death the unrealised—'To die will be an awfully big adventure!' 'I thought it was only flowers that died...
Perhaps she's frightened of being dead'—and, drawing
nearer to the particular, to build a hut, to live in a cave, to
foil pirates and redskins, mermaids and wolves, to sail a
ship, to be marooned... We have all been to our own
Never, Never Land and known its possibilities. This 'map
of a child's mind,' wrote Barrie, 'is always more or less an
island, with astonishing splashes of colour here and there,
and coral reefs and rakish-looking craft in the offing, and
savages and lonely lairs, and gnomes who are mostly
tailors, and caves through which a river runs, and princes
with six elder brothers, and a hut fast going to decay...'
The island has always room for more details: a corner of
Tarzan's jungle or a back entrance to Kôr, a scrap of lunar
landscape or a province of Narnia. But in its essentials it is
still the same and ever present, though Barrie alone of
mortals caught it for a magic moment and brought away a
reflection of it that nearly all of us can recognise.

Denis Mackail wrote of *Peter Pan*:

'Though he put his heart and soul and all his thoughts
into it, something deeper and still more individual had
actually guided his pen. An alchemy, as mysterious and
often as disturbing to him as to anyone else, which had
taken his own sadness and nostalgia for childhood, his games
with the little Davieses, and thirty years of constant if not
always conscious preoccupation with the stage, and had
turned them into dialogue and direction, and three hours
of magic, utterly different from anything yet known.'

The penalty of a great work of art is that as soon as it is written or acted everyone can say how obvious and inevitable, and even easy, it is: in other words, that the author has captured a corner of the universal experience which no one had set to words or music or canvas before. Thus it is difficult to realise how utterly new, original and different *Peter Pan* was when Barrie was ready to look for a manager in 1904.

The play, he knew, would be a complete gamble and yet demand many and costly settings, besides a company of about fifty. So, acting on the principle concerning which he punned later in *Rosy Rapture*: 'All Gaul is divided into Tree parts', he began by reading it to Beerbohm Tree, already famous for his fabulous productions at His Majesty's Theatre. But Tree was not amused, and even went so far as to warn Barrie's usual manager, the American impresario Charles Frohman, that this remarkable author had gone out of his mind.

But Frohman was so thrilled with *Peter Pan* that he set to work on it at once, sparing no expense, and introduced it to the world at the Duke of York's Theatre, London, on December 27, 1904, with five elaborate sets and two front-drops, with costumes by William Nicholson (but the first Peter Pan collar by Henry J. Ford, illustrator of the Andrew Lang Fairy Books) and with Nina Boucicault, Gerald du Maurier, Hilda Trevelyan and George Shelton as, it is generally agreed, the best Peter, Hook, Wendy and Smee in all the play's astonishing stage history.

The first night was packed, with a mainly adult audience, but the orchestra had no need to lead the clapping to save Tinker Bell's life; the critics (except Max Beerbohm) were laudatory, but there were, it is said, a few days of uncertainty. Then the play exerted its spell and drew young and old to pack its houses with enthusiasts, as it has continued to do from that day to this in more than twelve thousand performances in Great Britain alone. Perhaps fifteen million of us have seen *Peter Pan* during the last sixty years. It was as popular in America, Maude Adams as Peter touring for long periods besides reviving it several times in New York, where there have been several major productions of recent years, besides a number of seasons by Eva le Gallienne in the late twenties and early thirties. It has been translated and produced with success in France, Italy and Germany—and doubtless in many other countries too, both English-speaking and otherwise, of which no records are available.

The original production was by Dion Boucicault, brother of the first Peter Pan, and when the first run ended on April 1, 1905, it was announced that it would be resumed on December 19. Boucicault was in charge for many years, and was succeeded by his stage-manager Lichfield Owen, who in time handed on to Cecil King the same, original production, which only ended in 1954 after half a century. As clothes, props or scenery wore out, they were replaced by exact reproductions; some of the garments survived to the end, and Hook's original coat became an heirloom worn at least once by every one of Gerald du Maurier's successors.

Even the cast never changed completely. George Shelton, the original Smee, played the part for twenty-four years, while James English and John Kelt as Jukes and Noodler scored twenty-eight—only to be surpassed by William Luff, present holder of the record, with forty-five years between 1906 and 1953. 'I never want to see *Peter Pan* without Luff as Cecco,' said Barrie, and he can seldom have done so—with the notable exception of the 1927-8 revival, when Luff played Captain Hook throughout the London run, a part which, as official understudy, he played for short periods on many other occasions, and several times in the early tours.

As Hook, William Luff was surpassed by Lionel Gadsden, who played it for seventeen long tours (over 2,500 performances) in the period between 1913 and 1938, when a duplicate company opened in the provinces before Christmas and toured for an average of four months. For nearly all of us who saw *Peter Pan* outside London before 1935 Lionel Gadsden was the one and only Captain Hook. In his old age he returned to the play, twice as Great Big Little Panther, and from 1955 to 1961 as Noodler: at the age of eighty he was still able to give a fine performance as Hook when the principal fell ill.

These are only a few of the records: for example Peter Cotes has at various times played John, Slightly and Starkey; Jane Baxter has been a Redskin, Mrs Darling and Peter Pan, and so on. The most famous Peters have been Pauline Chase who played it for eight revivals and Jean Forbes-Robertson who played it for nine, but the list includes a galaxy of stars ranging from Fay Compton and Gladys Cooper to Ann Todd and Margaret Lockwood, just as, after du Maurier, we may select the most notable Hooks from Henry Ainley, Ralph Richardson, Alastair Sim, Charles Laughton and Donald Wolfit. Hilda Trevelyan has never been surpassed: 'You are Wendy and there will never be another to touch you,' wrote Barrie in 1920, and she played the part for nine seasons: those who saw her and have seen most of her successors award the second place to Joyce Redman. Only four actresses seem to have played both Wendy and Peter: Lila Maravan, Dinah Sheridan, Joan Greenwood and Julia Lockwood.

The only name that has never changed on any *Peter Pan* programme is that of Jane Wren (sometimes Jenny in the provinces) as Tinker Bell, even during the one season (1911) when a real actress, Anna Langley, played the part behind a 'minimising' glass. For Miss Wren (although she once received a demand note from H.M. Inspector of Taxes) is only the reflection of a spotlight from a tiny mirror in the stage-manager's hand, and her voice is a collar of bells and two special ones (to say 'You silly ass!') which Barrie brought from Switzerland.

The Peter Pan legend is not confined to the play. He did not only fly straight across the footlights and out into folk-lore and have his name taken in vain by innumerable makers of toys or clothes for the young. On May 1, 1912, his statue by Sir George Frampton appeared suddenly in Kensington Gardens, on the bank of the Serpentine where he first landed from the Thrush's Nest; and, more formally, Pauline Chase unveiled a replica in Liverpool in 1928.

She had already edited *Peter Pan's Postbag*, consisting of letters from children sent to Peter Pan himself at the Duke of York's Theatre, in 1909; and Wendy or Smee could boast almost as big a fan-mail. But Peter Pan was already being re-told in story form (notably by Daniel O'Connor and Mary Byron), and there were soon *The Peter Pan Alphabet—Painting Book—Keepsake*, and so on. In fact there are so many versions and variants of *Peter Pan* that Frank Eyre wrote in his *Twentieth Century Children's Books* in 1952 that,

'. . . only a portion of the children who read it do so in Barrie's own words, but the tale itself is such an inspired amalgam of a dozen familiar and inspired ingredients that it survives all adaptation. It may very well in the end be more likely to live as a traditional nursery story, told in innumerable versions, like *Cinderella* or *Little Red Riding Hood*, than as an individual piece of creative writing.'

The play was not published until 1928, when Barrie revised it considerably, and wrote many delightful stage directions, besides an amusing Introduction, the 'Dedication' to the Davies boys. However, in 1911 he had made the play into a book, *Peter and Wendy* (*Peter Pan and Wendy* in later editions); so good a book that it is surprising to find the short versions still being reissued. It is even stranger to find how comparatively little known the real book seems to be.

The style is not always easy for the child reader, and a few of the conceits are definitely of the adult Barrie variety; but these are only stray motes in the sunbeam. All the play is digested into the story, and much more besides, with a finality and a conviction that only Barrie could achieve. All the questions are answered, too, including what happened 'When Wendy Grew Up', which Barrie wrote first as an additional scene to the play, *An Afterthought*, which was acted for a single performance (February 22, 1908) and published for the first time in its original form in 1957. Altogether *Peter Pan and Wendy* is a perfect book for children, and children who find it at the right age are engrossed by it and remember it vividly. It should be better known, and would gain by appearing in some popular edition, and certainly with worthy illustrations: in this respect it has never been well served.

Barrie wrote another version of *Peter Pan* which is the least known of any: a scenario for a silent film that was never made. This waif of the Never, Never Land, which was first published in 1954 in the present author's *Fifty Years of 'Peter Pan'*, can stand comparison unflinchingly with Peter Pan's other two media, and contains many delightful touches and intriguing suggestions not to be found in either but every bit as genuine and authentic.

Though Barrie's scenario was not used, a silent film of *Peter Pan* appeared in 1924, little more than an uninspired imitation of the play. Walt Disney turned the story into a coloured cartoon film in 1953 and achieved a much more worthy result, proving in his own way that the legend can stand on its own without much help from Barrie, though only as a thrilling game with the deeper magic in abeyance.

Meanwhile the play is still revived each Christmas and continues to pack houses twice daily for five weeks in London and ten in the provinces. In 1954 a completely new production was launched, with many cuts in the script so as to allow the central act, 'The Mermaid's Lagoon', to return from many years of exile. Superb sets and costumes, intelligent, and for the last few years a loving, production, and a dashing sense of excitement more than compensate for what has been lost, and make of it a new revelation and a new joy. Only something of the magic is missing, since no Peter seems able to catch the eeriness of Nina Boucicault or the intangible and fey quality of Jean Forbes-Robertson, and some of the key lines have gone in consequence. Some also of the lines that evoke the underlying depth have disappeared, the shadow of tragedy in the background which for the adult theatre-goer makes *Peter Pan* something more than the best play for children ever written.

IV. Lob's Wood

Barrie, wrote the *Observer's* leader-writer the day after his death, was 'a romantic who could suddenly turn round and write the realists off the stage. It is customary nowadays to make fun of his excursions into fairyland. That he made greater excursions elsewhere is too easily forgotten.'

Although *Peter Pan* stands alone and, taken as a whole conception, is one of the few supreme contributions to children's literature,* it is not his only great work. Without it, indeed, he would probably hold at this moment a much higher place as a dramatist, or at least be taken more seriously as such. Writers of the greatest works for children seem to have become the natural prey of the psycho-analysts, and Barrie even more than Lewis Carroll or Kenneth Grahame has proved an irresistible target for their attentions. There seems to have been more excuse for their interest in his case than in either of the others, for the 'mark set on a boy's soul' by Margaret Ogilvy was never quite obliterated, and the failure of his marriage with the divorce of his wife on an adultery charge in 1909 suggests that there was something of autobiography in Grizel's quandary:

'He did not love her. "Not as I love him", she said to herself. "Not as married people ought to love, but in the other way he loves me dearly." By the other way she meant that he loved her as he loved Elspeth [his sister], and loved

---

* F. J. Harvey Darton in his *Children's Books in England* (1932), the standard work on the subject, wrote of *Peter Pan* that it 'has influenced the spirit of children's books, and the grown-up view of them, more powerfully than any other work except the *Alices* and Andersen's *Fairy Tales*'.

them both just as he had loved them when all three played in the den. He was a boy who could not grow up.'

Such handicaps, and whatever of tragedy comes from them, should be the private concern of the sufferer only; however, inevitably in the case of an author they have some effect on his work and are deemed to be of public interest. But while the psychological background may help to form a work of art, it is false logic to assume that the work of art is rendered unhealthy by any oddness in the spiritual equipment of the author. Because Barrie was endowed with an abnormal power of re-entering his childhood, it must not be thought that the childhood he depicted in his writings was therefore abnormal: it is not the past that is morbid, but the desire to escape too often into it. Whatever Barrie's own experience may have been, or however great his temptation, all that concerns us is the work of art that results. *Peter Pan* can be accepted fully by the child: it is childhood enjoyed to the full, as each age and experience should be. Barrie might just as well be accused of a 'middle-age' complex for writing his one-act play *Rosalind* (1912) in which the middle-aged actress, Beatrice Page, escapes from her artificial youthfulness in theatrical life to revel in every detail of her actual age when on holiday.

Peter Pan was always, to Barrie, 'the tragic boy', and the tragedy is plain for the adult reader or theatre-goer. But a children's play was not the play for 'writing the realists off the stage'.

Barrie took, as it were, a breathing space after *Peter Pan*, with the slight and rather artificial full-length play *Alice-Sit-by-the-Fire* (1905), two whimsical scraps of gossamer, the one-act 'toy tragedies' of *Pantaloon* (1905) and *Punch* (1906) and the topical and completely ephemeral revue sketch, *Josephine* (1906), before writing one of his most enduring plays, *What Every Woman Knows* (1908). This is realism as a fine art, quiet satire and deep understanding of humanity, dressed in all the outward charm and graciousness of which he was a master: it shares with *The Admirable Crichton* the distinction of being the most acceptable of his plays to the present prosaic age.

Little work of note appeared for some years after this. A period of depression followed the divorce in 1909, and much of his time was given up to the five sons of Arthur and Sylvia Llewelyn Davies, the child-friends of Kensington Gardens and Black Lake, whom he began to help when their father died unexpectedly in 1907, and adopted completely in 1910 on their mother's death. When troubles came, Barrie tended to shut himself away from even his closest friends, but the depression did not last, and it is a mistake to think of him as the lonely, tormented soul with a morbid bias towards pessimism, which is the impression that some of his biographers tend to leave with us.

One of his adopted sons writes:

'My memory of Barrie, if it has its portion of melancholy, is heavily tilted towards fun and incomparable sparkle. He was a man of extremes and when he was sad he was sadder than death; but so far at any rate as I was concerned, ninety per cent of the time he was an irresistible delight.'

In fact, with his intensely introspective and imaginative temperament, he was like his own Beatrice Page as Charles describes her in *Rosalind*: 'If you weren't all glee you were the saddest thing on earth.' And sad or gleeful, he was intensely generous, and ready always with help where it was most needed, and nearly always so unostentatiously that the majority of his benefactions remain unknown. Of those which could not be hidden the gift of all rights and royalties in *Peter Pan* to the Great Ormond Street Hospital for Sick Children in 1929 is the most famous. There were many others during the Great War of 1914–18, beginning with the hospital at Wrest Park (which finds a place in *A Kiss for Cinderella*) and the more famous one at Bettancourt in France, and exemplified in the sketches and playlets which he wrote for charity performances, such as *The Fatal Typist* (1915), *Shakespeare's Legacy* (1916), *Reconstructing the Crime* (1917), and *La Politesse* (1918)—trifles long forgotten, but guaranteed to bring packed houses to swell the funds of the good causes for which they were given.

After 1908 one-act plays were, for some time, all that Barrie had to offer: *Old Friends*, *The Twelve-Pound Look* (both 1910), *Rosalind* (1912), and *Half an Hour* and *The Will* in 1913. In that year the next full-length play appeared, Barrie's one complete failure, *The Adored One* (acted with a little more success in America as *The Legend of Leonora*). The brilliant first act was afterwards made into a separate 'curtain-raiser' as *Seven Women*; but the rest is rightly buried in oblivion—the only case where the whimsy of which he is so often accused is so much in evidence as to get the better of his sense of theatre.

With the outbreak of war, Barrie turned his mind to the entertainment of the troops on leave, and attempted a full-scale revue, called *Rosy Rapture*: slight but amusing, with ample scope for the chorus headed by the beautiful Gaby Deslys, round whom the trifle of plot was built, but little of the true Barrie in it.

The next real play, *A Kiss for Cinderella* (March 16, 1916), dates a little, or has not quite become a period piece; but the central scene of Cinderella's dream, 'The Ball at the Palace' as a little London slum child would imagine it, is quite ageless, and a delightful memory for those of us who

175

are lucky enough to have seen the play as children. There have been several revivals in London, and many by repertory companies; but it has slipped out of fashion lately, and is overdue for a return. It is not, of course, in the same class as *Peter Pan*, but high on our meagre list of children's stage classics.

The one-act plays also continued, now with some reference to the War in them, such as *Der Tag* (1914), *The New Word* (1915), *The Old Lady Shows Her Medals* (1917), and *A Well-Remembered Voice* (1918). But in 1917 Barrie felt that he had used up all his good ideas and would never write a first-class play again. He was living by now in his high flat in Adelphi Terrace overlooking the Thames, and in February of that year his friend A. E. W. Mason, on leave from the Secret Service, came to stay with him. Many years afterwards, Mason wrote:

'I have the clearest possible recollection of that episode. I was in Barrie's flat, in bed for a week with bronchitis deepening into pneumonia. During that week Barrie told me that he was worried because he could not think of any subject to work upon. I said that I remembered that before his divorce he had begun on what I thought was probably the best theme he had ever struck—that of a group of people who were always saying: "Oh! if we could begin again!" And they did begin again and did exactly as they had done the first time. Barrie had forgotten all about it . . . He sat down to work practically at once.'

Dear Brutus ('The fault, dear Brutus, is not in our stars, but in ourselves') was finished in a few months and had its first night on October 17, 1917, after which it ran for 365 performances and has had three successful revivals in the West End, besides innumerable touring, repertory and amateur productions. This excursion into fairyland in search of the deepest realism is held by many to be Barrie's greatest play, and is certainly the most typical and shows his genius at its highest peak. Although described as a comedy, there are undertones of tragedy as the couples slip out into Lob's Wood to have their second chance, only to make the same choice as before as they pass before us, their secret selves revealed, in the magic moonlight; yet in the last act they find the quiet and sufficient philosophy of acceptance of things as they have turned out. Only for Dearth, who has found his dream-daughter in the Wood, is there real tragedy, but for him most of all there is hope, since for the Dearths alone of the party the might-have-been is still the might-be which is 'only for the brave ones'. When all seems over, the Dearths pass across the stage outside the window hand in hand, looking not to the past but to the future. And Margaret the dream-child steals timidly across behind them.

'Barrie with a plot and Barrie expressing a philosophy on which he had mused for years,' wrote Denis Mackail, 'and, in its own mood and convention, as near as almost nothing to a flawless play.'

He could not quite repeat his success, though *Mary Rose* (April 22, 1920) had an even more overwhelming reception, ran longer, had books written about it and was twice revived within its first ten years. But the story, based on the old Scottish legends or folk-tales of mortals who have disappeared into fairyland for many years and returned not a day older and with no memory of the missing years, lacks the underlying philosophy which in *Dear Brutus* overcomes the essentially modern reaction against any mixture of realism and the marvellous. *Mary Rose* captured and held spellbound large audiences for many hundreds of performances; but we can only take their word for its absolutely magical effect as a theatrical experience, since it has not appeared on the

London stage for over thirty years and would certainly need superlative acting and production to achieve its full effect.

This was Barrie's last play for sixteen years. He had already written the first act of a murder play, so brilliantly constructed that it seemed impossible to work it out through the subsequent acts. That he would have done so is not open to doubt, but he was writing it very much at the insistence of the favourite among his adopted sons, Michael Davies who was still an undergraduate at Oxford. On May 19, 1921, Michael was bathing in a favourite but dangerous pool at Sandford Lasher and was dragged down into the race of the weir: his friend Rupert Buxton tried to save him, but both were drowned.

Michael's death was the worst blow Barrie ever received. 'He never got over it,' says Mr Mackail. 'It altered and darkened everything for the rest of his life.' Certainly he had no heart to continue and to finish the play, but it was acted again and again as *Shall We Join the Ladies?*—one of the most perfect of curtain-raisers.

Barrie wrote little more, but during the next ten years he cultivated the art of oratory, and became celebrated as a public speaker. His best known speech, *Courage*, made when he was Lord Rector of St Andrews University, was published separately in 1922; but the posthumous volume, *M'Connachie and J.M.B.* (1938), contains many more as well worth reading.

A selection of his early articles, mainly from *The St James's Gazette*, served him for the basis of a pleasant volume of reminiscences, *The Greenwood Hat*, printed privately in 1930 and published in 1937. A short story *Neil and Tintinnabulum: An Interlude for Parents*, contributed in 1925 to *The Flying Carpet*, a collection of children's stories edited by his secretary Lady Cynthia Asquith, showed little of the old inspiration. But in 1931 appeared *Farewell, Miss Julie Logan*, a long short story harking back suddenly to the neighbourhood of Kirriemuir, but with all the skill of construction and compression that he had lacked in the days of the Thrums novels: perfect of its kind, full of wistful charm, and a worthy pendant to his life's work.

Then suddenly in 1934 a chance suggestion from a new star actress, Elisabeth Bergner, set Barrie writing his last and most unexpected play. *The Boy David* was neither like anything he had written, nor like anything that was being written. Its production was accompanied by an almost sensational run of bad luck, and it finally reached London at a time when all thoughts were fixed on the abdication of King Edward VIII, was put on in far too big a theatre and in too lavish a style, and lacked Barrie's presence, owing to illness, at the final rehearsals and the trial run to packed houses in Edinburgh.

'A marvellous piece of philosophic and mystic thinking and creation,' wrote Rosaline Masson after the first night. 'I don't think "Shakespearean" is an exaggerated term to use.' But the London critics in December 1936 thought otherwise, and the vastness of His Majesty's Theatre was only crammed when it was announced that the play was about to be withdrawn.

Yet, though the plot falters during the visions in the third act, Barrie's picture of David in the days before he became King of Israel has a stage magic and a wistful poetry entirely its own, and these come across perfectly in a small theatre and an intimate production.

Barrie was a dying man when the original production came to an end after only fifty-five performances, and the disappointment was severe. He died quietly on June 19,

1937, aged seventy-seven, and was buried with his own people in a simple grave in the cemetery at Kirriemuir.

'When a great man dies,' wrote Barrie after the death of George Meredith, 'the immortals await him at the top of the nearest hill.' With them the author of *Dear Brutus* and *The Admirable Crichton* would be sure of his place even if he had not written *Peter Pan*. This, his most enduring creation, gives him as assured a niche near the top of another summit. On the drop curtain (painted to look like an old sampler sewn by Wendy) which he designed for *Peter Pan* he wrote, 'Dear Hans Christian Andersen. Dear Charles Lamb. Dear Lewis Carroll. Dear Robert Louis Stevenson.' We may without hesitation add, 'Dear J. M. Barrie.'

BIBLIOGRAPHY

Bibliography

I. BOOKS
(other than plays)

Better Dead. Swan Sonnenschein, 1888 [1887].

Auld Licht Idylls. Hodder and Stoughton, 1888.

When a Man's Single. Hodder and Stoughton, 1888.

An Edinburgh Eleven : Pen Portraits from College Life. Hodder and Stoughton, 1889.

A Window in Thrums. Hodder and Stoughton, 1889.

My Lady Nicotine. Hodder and Stoughton, 1890.

The Little Minister. Cassell, 1891.

A Tillyloss Scandal. Lovell, [1893]. *Two of Them.* Lovell, 1893. Unauthorised collections of stories and sketches, published only in U.S.A. (There were other such volumes, but these two contain most of the pieces included in them).

Margaret Ogilvy. Hodder and Stoughton, 1896.

Sentimental Tommy. Cassell, 1896.

Tommy and Grizel. Cassell, 1900.

The Little White Bird. Hodder and Stoughton, 1902.

Peter Pan in Kensington Gardens. Hodder and Stoughton, 1906. (Reprinted chapters from *The Little White Bird*).

Peter and Wendy. Hodder and Stoughton, 1911.

Farewell, Miss Julie Logan. Hodder and Stoughton, 1932.

The Greenwood Hat. [Privately printed 1930]. Peter Davies, 1937.

M'Connachie and J.M.B. : Speeches by J. M. Barrie. Peter Davies, 1938.

Letters of J. M. Barrie. (Edited by Viola Meynell). Peter Davies, 1942.

II. PLAYS
(other than revue sketches and ephemera)

[One-act plays are indicated by an asterisk *. Final date is of first publication; where none is given, the play remains unpublished. Those followed by the letter [C] are included in *The Definitive Edition of the Plays of J. M. Barrie*, 1942. The plays were published by Hodder and Stoughton, except where other publishers are given].

*Caught Napping. [Never acted]. 1883. [Privately Printed].

Richard Savage [with H. B. Marriott Watson]. (Criterion, April 16, 1891). 1891. [Privately Printed].

*Ibsen's Ghost. (Toole's Theatre, May 30, 1891).

Walker, London. (Toole's Theatre, February 25, 1892). Samuel French, 1907. [C].

Jane Annie, or The Good Conduct Prize. [Libretto in collaboration with A. Conan Doyle]. (Savoy, May 13, 1893). Chappell, 1893.

The Professor's Love Story. (Star [New York], December 19, 1892; Comedy [London], June 26, 1894). [C].

The Little Minister (Haymarket, November 6, 1897). [C].

The Wedding Guest. (Garrick, September 27, 1900). *Fortnightly Review*, 1900. [C].

Quality Street. (Vaudeville, September 17, 1902). 1913. [C].

The Admirable Crichton. (Duke of York's, November 4, 1902). 1914. [C].

Little Mary. (Wyndham's, September 24, 1903). [C].

Peter Pan. (Duke of York's, December 27, 1904). 1928. [C].

*Pantaloon. (Duke of York's, April 5, 1905). 1914. [C].

Alice-Sit-by-the-Fire. (Duke of York's, April 5, 1905). 1919. [C].

*Punch. (Comedy, April 5, 1906).

*When Wendy Grew Up: An Afterthought. (Duke of York's, February 22, 1908). Nelson, 1957.

What Every Woman Knows. (Duke of York's, September 3, 1908). 1918. [C].

*Old Friends. (Duke of York's, March 1, 1910). 1928. [C].

*The Twelve-Pound Look. (Duke of York's, March 1, 1910). 1914. [C].

*A Slice of Life. (Duke of York's, June 7, 1910).

*Rosalind. (Duke of York's, October 14, 1912). 1914. [C].

*The Will. (Duke of York's, September 4, 1913). 1914. [C].

The Adored One. (Duke of York's, September 4, 1913). [Revised as *The Legend of Leonora*, Empire, New York, January 5, 1914].

*Half an Hour. (Hippodrome, September 29, 1913). 1928. [C].
*Der Tag. (Coliseum, December 21, 1914). 1914.
*The New Word. (Duke of York's, March 22, 1915). 1918. [C].
Rosy Rapture. [Revue]. (Duke of York's, March 22, 1915).
A Kiss for Cinderella. (Wyndham's, March 16, 1916). 1920. [C.]
*Seven Women. (New, April 7, 1917). 1928. [C].
*The Old Lady Shows Her Medals. (New, April 7, 1917). 1918. [C].
Dear Brutus. (Wyndham's, October 17, 1917). 1923. [C].
*A Well-Remembered Voice. (Wyndham's, June 28, 1918). 1918. [C].
*Barbara's Wedding. (Savoy, August 23, 1927). 1918. [C].
*The Truth About the Russian Dancers. (Coliseum, March 16, 1920). N.Y. 1962.
Mary Rose. (Haymarket, April 22, 1920). 1924. [C].
*Shall We Join the Ladies? (R.A.D.A., May 27, 1921). 1927. [C].
The Boy David. (His Majesty's, November 21, 1936). Peter Davies, 1938. [C].

---

*The Fight for Mr Lapraik. [Written 1917. No professional production]. 1947 (in New Plays Quarterly).
Scenario for a Silent Film of 'Peter Pan'. [Written 1920. Not used. First published in Roger Lancelyn Green's Fifty Years of 'Peter Pan', Peter Davies, 1954].

Half Hours, published 1914, contained Pantaloon, The Twelve-Pound Look, Rosalind, and The Will.
Echoes of the War, published 1918, contained The Old Lady Shows Her Medals, The New Word, Barbara's Wedding and A Well-Remembered Voice.
Shall We Join the Ladies? and Other Plays, published 1928, also contained Half an Hour, Seven Women and Old Friends.
The Definitive Edition of the Plays of J. M. Barrie in one volume [plays marked [C] in list above] was published by Hodder and Stoughton in 1942. (The first Collected Edition in 1928 contained six fewer full-length plays).

J. M. Barrie's Plays and Stories. Edited by Roger Lancelyn
Green. Everyman Library, 1962. [Contains *The Admirable
Crichton, Dear Brutus, Shall We Join the Ladies?*, *Courage*,
'T'nowhead's Bell', and *Farewell, Miss Julie Logan*.]

III. MISCELLANEOUS WRITINGS

A. Pamphlets and Speeches.
Allahakbarries C.C. [Privately printed]. 1893.
Scotland's Lament : A Poem on the Death of R. L. Stevenson. (*The
Bookman*, January 1895, and as privately printed pamphlet).
1895.
The Allahakbarrie Book of Broadway Cricket. [Privately printed].
1899. Published (as *Allahakbarries C.C. 1899*). James Barrie,
1950.
George Meredith. Constable, 1909.
Charles Frohman : A Tribute. (*Daily Mail*, May 10, and privately
printed pamphlet). 1915.
Courage. [Speech at St Andrews, May 3, 1922]. Hodder and
Stoughton, 1922.
The Entrancing Life. [Speech at Edinburgh, October 25, 1930].
Hodder and Stoughton, 1930.

B. Contributions to Books by other writers include
Preface to R. M. Ballantyne's *The Coral Island*. James Nisbet,
1913.
Introduction to Charles Turley's *The Voyages of Captain Scott*.
Smith, Elder, 1914.
Preface to Daisy Ashford's *The Young Visiters*. Chatto and Win-
dus, 1919.
'Neil and Tintinnabulum'. *The Flying Carpet*. Edited by Cynthia
Asquith. Partridge, 1925.
'The Blot on Peter Pan'. *The Treasure Ship*. Edited by Cynthia
Asquith. Partridge, 1926.

C. Theatrical Miscellanea. All unpublished
Becky Sharp. [One-act adaptation from *Vanity Fair*]. (Terry's
Theatre, June 3, 1893).
A Platonic Friendship. [Duologue]. (Drury Lane, March 17, 1898).
Josephine. [Revue in three scenes]. (Comedy, April 5, 1906).

The Dramatists Get What They Wanted. [One-act burlesque].
   (Hippodrome, December 23, 1912).
The Ladies' Shakespeare. [One-act burlesque]. (Hamilton, Ont.,
   Canada, October 26, 1914).
The Fatal Typist. [Playlet for charity]. (His Majesty's, November
   19, 1915).
The Real Thing At Last. [Short burlesque film]. (Coliseum,
   February 7, 1916).
Shakespeare's Legacy. [Playlet for charity]. (Drury Lane, April
   14, 1916). [Privately printed 1916].
Reconstructing the Crime. [Entertainment for charity]. (Palace,
   February 16, 1917).
The Origin of Harlequin. [Ballet]. (Palace, February 16, 1917;
   Wyndhams, June 28, 1918).
La Politesse. [Playlet for charity]. (Wyndhams, June 28, 1918).

D. *Private Entertainments* (*usually acted for or by children*).
   All unpublished
Bandelero the Bandit. (Dumfries Amateur Dramatic Club, 1877).
The Greedy Dwarf. (133 Gloucester Road, January 7, 1901).
The Cinema Supper. (Scala Theatre, July 3, 1914).
Where Was Simon? (Stanway, Gloucestershire: January 16, 1926).
The Wheel: A Play for Eight Children and their Grandpapa.
   (Stanway, April 18, 1927).

IV. BOOKS ABOUT J. M. BARRIE

J. M. Barrie and His Books: Biographical and Critical Studies by
   J. A. Hammerton. Horace Marshall, 1900.
J. M. Barrie and the Theatre by H. M. Walbrook. F. V. White
   & Co., 1922.
J. M. Barrie: A Study in Fairies and Mortals by Patrick Bray-
   brooke. Drane's, 1924.
A New Approach to an Analysis of 'Mary Rose' by P. L. Geitein,
   1926.
Barrie by Thomas Moult. Jonathan Cape, 1928.
*A Bibliography of the Writings of Sir James Matthew Barrie, Bart,
   O.M.,* by Herbert Garland. Bookman's Journal, 1928.
Barrie: The Story of a Genius by J. A. Hammerton. Sampson,
   Low, 1929.

J. M. Barrie by F. J. Harvey Darton. Nisbet, 1929.

Sir James Barrie als Dramatiker by W. Eschenauer. 1930.

Thrums and the Barrie Country by John Kennedy. Heath Cranton, 1930.

Sir James M. Barrie : A Bibliography by B. D. Cutler [New York], 1931.

Sir J. M. Barrie : His First Editions by Andrew Block. Foyle, 1933.

James Matthew Barrie : an Appreciation by James A. Roy. Jarrolds, 1937.

The Barrie Inspiration by Patrick Chalmers. Peter Davies, 1938.

J. M. Barrie by W. A. Darlington. Blackie, 1938.

The Story of J.M.B. : A Biography by Denis Mackail. Peter Davies, 1941.

Barrie and the Kailyard School by George Blake. Arthur Barker, 1951.

Fifty Years of 'Peter Pan' by Roger Lancelyn Green. Peter Davies, 1954.

Portrait of Barrie by Cynthia Asquith. James Barrie, 1954.

V. A FEW BOOKS CONTAINING
SECTIONS OF PARTICULAR BARRIE INTEREST

Peter Pan's Postbag edited by Pauline Chase. Heinemann, 1909.

Charles Frohman by I. F. Marcossin and D. Frohman. The Bodley Head, 1916.

Essays on Modern Dramatists by W. L. Phelps. (New York) 1921.

It's Smee by George Shelton. Ernest Benn, 1928.

Gerald : A Portrait by Daphne du Maurier. Gollancz, 1934.

Dear Turly : contribution by Cynthia Asquith. Frederick Muller, 1942.

To Tell My Story by Irene Vanburgh. Hutchinson, 1948.

Through Stage Doors by Sydney Blow [and Hilda Trevelyan]. Chambers, 1958.